Accessibility Handbook
Making 508 Websites for Everyone

Katie Cunningham

O'REILLY®

Beijing · Cambridge · Farnham · Köln · Sebastopol · Tokyo

Accessibility Handbook
by Katie Cunningham

Published by O'Reilly Media, Inc., 1005 Gravenstein Highway North, Sebastopol, CA 95472.

O'Reilly books may be purchased for educational, business, or sales promotional use. Online editions are also available for most titles (*http://my.safaribooksonline.com*). For more information, contact our corporate/institutional sales department: 800-998-9938 or *corporate@oreilly.com*.

Editors: Julie Steele and Meghan Blanchette	**Cover Designer:** Karen Montgomery
Production Editor: Rachel Steely	**Interior Designer:** David Futato
Proofreader: Melanie Yarbrough	**Illustrators:** Robert Romano and Rebecca Demarest

Revision History for the First Edition:
   2012-08-24   First release
See *http://oreilly.com/catalog/errata.csp?isbn=9781449322854* for release details.

Table of Contents

Preface

How I Got into Accessibility

Many people ask me how a developer who was working on the back-end for websites got involved in accessibility. After all, it wasn't technically a part of my job description. It wasn't going to make our sites faster (though I later found out it could have that side affect). I didn't have a disability, nor did I seem to be closely associated with the disabled.

The truth of the matter: I stumbled into it. I was working on a contract at NASA, and we were required to make our sites 508 compliant in order to get them deployed. A separate group was responsible for assessing our sites then sending us exact fixes. Our websites kept failing and we found ourselves falling behind schedule again and again.

We often asked the testers to explain why something had failed, but they, like everyone else on the contract, were too busy to take time to educate a handful of developers. They gave us a checklist, which we read and were baffled by. Tables need scopes? What are scopes? Why do they need them? What's wrong with the designer's color scheme? What do you mean the contrast is no good? Why was our alt text rejected?

At the time, the resources on the Internet focused on more on policy makers and lawyers than developers. Though we found many tips about creating an accessible application, few included why these added tags made our sites easier for the disabled to use. This made it increasingly difficult to make websites that were new and innovative without wondering if we were inadvertently shutting someone out.

Why This Book?

Though there are books that talk about 508 compliance, few focused on the people that do the actual development. They were for managers or testers, and offered few practical insights into the world of accessibility.

It took me years of battling testers, Googling, and playing with tools to get a full understanding of accessibility. I didn't think it should be that hard, though. Why couldn't all of this information be collected in one place so I could take it in within a few sittings?

Why did I have to wait for issues to come up before researching how to fix them? How could we develop new technologies without patching them later for accessibility?

I decided to write a book that focused on the disabilities rather than the patches. Yes, alt text should always be used and tables should always be scoped. What's even more important to understand is how poor alt text or tables with no scopes affect the experience of a user. Understanding a user's tools and limitations helps developers and designers make the next generation of web applications without excluding anyone.

I've also come to believe that making a site accessible makes it more usable for everyone. Though a few recommendations are exclusively for the disabled (such as alt text), many suggestions that will be made throughout the book will positively affect all users. No one likes forms that require absolute precision, and bad color choices hurt everyone. Creating a site that grows gracefully helps those on smaller monitors, such as tablets or netbooks, and including web fonts instead of images with text can make your site download faster. Good accessibility is good usability.

What Does It Mean to Be "Accessible"?

Being accessible is about making your website, with all of its data and functions, available for anyone, no matter how they have to use your website, or what difficulties they might have. Some people might have to use a screen reader, where the content of a site is read to them. Others may rely on subtitles and transcripts for audio content. Still others may be unable to use a mouse, or they may be using an adaptive device that works only through the mouse. They may need to override a website's styling in order to make it more readable for them.

In short, no one should be excluded from using your website simply because they have to access the Web in a different way.

Being accessible doesn't mean stripping your website of any advanced functions because someone is using a screen reader, or might have issues using a mouse. It doesn't mean a return to the days of unstyled web pages, or hiring a group of people dedicated to making your products accessible. Accessibility, if kept firmly in mind during development, can be done without significantly increasing overhead, and can even improve your website for your standard users.

Background of Section 508

In 1998, Congress passed an amendment to the Rehabilitation Act, requiring that all websites created for the United States government be accessible to everyone, in spite of individual handicaps. This amendment was Section 508, so often, web accessibility is referred to as "508 compliance." While the original act (passed in 1973) had its own 508 section in regards to technology, it was toothless until 1998, when standards were introduced. It was determined that any website paid for by federal funds must follow the requirements laid out in this amendment.

An out was written into the section, allowing for websites to get a waiver if their audience was small, and confirmed to have no one with any disabilities. With the growing number of disabled joining the ranks of not only the government, but also its contractors and affiliates, these waivers are growing more rare. It's difficult to prove that your audience will never include anyone with a disability, so this waiver is usually limited to top-secret projects or projects with an extremely limited timeframe (such as a workshop or one-time meeting).

Who Does It Cover?

The act covers anyone with a disability, but its interpretations often focus on three main groups:

- The visually impaired
- Those with hearing impairments
- Those with physical impairments

Why not just call the first two groups the blind and the deaf? Section 508 takes a broader stance, considering those with low-vision and color blindness, as well as those who may not be completely deaf.

Who Benefits from Accessibility?

Obviously, the main benefactors are those with vision or hearing issues, or who have physical limitations. As websites grew in complexity, many people in these groups were left behind. Tables used for layout kept screen readers from performing correctly. Complex layouts refused to grow gracefully, causing issues for people with low vision. Menus that dropped down, then snapped back at the slightest wavering of the cursor caused websites to be impossible to navigate for the motion impaired.

They're not the only benefactors, however. A website that is accessible for the disabled often gains the benefit of becoming easier to use for everyone. Narrow clicking margins are annoying to those with full mouse control as well as those with motion disorders. Websites that don't grow gracefully can be difficult for people using different size monitors. Someone on a low bandwidth connection (for example, tethered to a phone with a low data cap) might need to turn off images while surfing.

Also, it's important to remember that not everyone who is disabled has been disabled forever or will remain disabled. A person who has broken her dominant arm learns very quickly how difficult websites can be to navigate without a steady mouse. A person without headphones will have trouble with websites that require sound. And a person who has forgotten his glasses will be subjected to websites that don't deal with large text gracefully.

In other words, everyone can benefit in the end.

Who Is This Book for?

This book is centered around how to make a website accessible from a practical perspective rather than from a legal perspective. As such, this book is geared toward developers, both at the application and front-end layers, who wish to make their websites accessible. It's also presented as a way for those who manage projects to think about how they might work accessibility into their schedule, and how they might sell it to their customers. This book can also be used by quality assurance professionals interested in how to use testing tools for accessibility beyond tools that only scan HTML and look for obvious errors.

This book can also be used by those who wish to sell accessibility to customers who may not see the immediate benefits of making their website accessible. The last chapter is dedicated to collecting all the direct and indirect benefits of a focus on accessibility, while also making the case that doing so doesn't add as much overhead as some might fear.

Structure of This Book

Part of understanding accessibility is understanding the struggles of those with disabilities trying to use a website. For this reason, this book is split up into sections based on the disabilities covered in Section 508. Each section focuses on the specific challenges of the people with that disability, the tools they might use to work with their issues, and how a developer can make their life easier.

About Code Samples

Every effort has been made to make code samples that are clear, and reasonably cross-browser. The code samples should not be considered the end solution for the developer, however. Accessibility can be achieved in many ways, and the best solution is one that works with both the vision of the designer and the needs of all the users.

Each sample has been tested with the following browsers in Table P-1.

Table P-1. Browsers tested

Browser	Operating System	Versions
Internet Explorer	Windows	8+
Firefox	Windows	7+

Browser	Operating System	Versions
Chrome	Windows	10+
Firefox	Mac	7+
Safari	Mac	5+
Chromium	Unix	10+
Firefox	Unix	10+

With each example, only one solution is shown. While most of these should work with most modern browsers, the code is shown only as a guideline. As new technologies become more common, new solutions can be written. Years ago, formatting was done with tables because CSS wasn't common. These days, CSS is so common that using tables for layout seems archaic.

Conventions Used in This Book

The following typographical conventions are used in this book:

Italic
:   Indicates new terms, URLs, email addresses, filenames, and file extensions.

`Constant width`
:   Used for program listings, as well as within paragraphs to refer to program elements such as variable or function names, databases, data types, environment variables, statements, and keywords.

`Constant width bold`
:   Shows commands or other text that should be typed literally by the user.

`Constant width italic`
:   Shows text that should be replaced with user-supplied values or by values determined by context.

 This icon signifies a tip, suggestion, or general note.

 This icon indicates a warning or caution.

Using Code Examples

This book is here to help you get your job done. In general, you may use the code in this book in your programs and documentation. You do not need to contact us for permission unless you're reproducing a significant portion of the code. For example, writing a program that uses several chunks of code from this book does not require permission. Selling or distributing a CD-ROM of examples from O'Reilly books does require permission. Answering a question by citing this book and quoting example code does not require permission. Incorporating a significant amount of example code from this book into your product's documentation does require permission.

We appreciate, but do not require, attribution. An attribution usually includes the title, author, publisher, and ISBN. For example: "*Accessibility Handbook* by Katie Cunningham (O'Reilly). Copyright 2012 Katie Cunningham, 978-1-449-32285-4."

If you feel your use of code examples falls outside fair use or the permission given above, feel free to contact us at *permissions@oreilly.com*.

Safari® Books Online

Safari Books Online (*www.safaribooksonline.com*) is an on-demand digital library that delivers expert content in both book and video form from the world's leading authors in technology and business.

Technology professionals, software developers, web designers, and business and creative professionals use Safari Books Online as their primary resource for research, problem solving, learning, and certification training.

Safari Books Online offers a range of product mixes and pricing programs for organizations, government agencies, and individuals. Subscribers have access to thousands of books, training videos, and prepublication manuscripts in one fully searchable database from publishers like O'Reilly Media, Prentice Hall Professional, Addison-Wesley Professional, Microsoft Press, Sams, Que, Peachpit Press, Focal Press, Cisco Press, John Wiley & Sons, Syngress, Morgan Kaufmann, IBM Redbooks, Packt, Adobe Press, FT Press, Apress, Manning, New Riders, McGraw-Hill, Jones & Bartlett, Course Technology, and dozens more. For more information about Safari Books Online, please visit us online.

How to Contact Us

Please address comments and questions concerning this book to the publisher:

O'Reilly Media, Inc.
1005 Gravenstein Highway North
Sebastopol, CA 95472
800-998-9938 (in the United States or Canada)

707-829-0515 (international or local)
707-829-0104 (fax)

We have a web page for this book, where we list errata, examples, and any additional information. You can access this page at *http://oreil.ly/access_handbook*.

To comment or ask technical questions about this book, send email to *bookquestions@oreilly.com*.

For more information about our books, courses, conferences, and news, see our website at *http://www.oreilly.com*.

Find us on Facebook: *http://facebook.com/oreilly*

Follow us on Twitter: *http://twitter.com/oreillymedia*

Watch us on YouTube: *http://www.youtube.com/oreillymedia*

Acknowledgments

I'd like to thank my first editor, Julie Steele, for recognizing that this was a book that was needed. I'd also like to thank my second editor, Meghan Blanchette, for her never-ending patience while I struggled to finish the book.

Without my husband, Jim, I never would have been able to finish the book. He gave me space when I needed to write, wrangled the kids, brought me food when I needed to eat, and poured me wine when I needed to chill.

And kids? Thank you for learning that headphones mean that it's a bad time to poke your mother.

And finally, I had the best tech editors in the world. They made this book so much stronger by being involved with it. Doug Hellman, Tom Wolber, Scot Taylor, and Sean O'Connor: You guys are the best!

Complete Blindness

Since the Internet is a visual medium, it should come as no surprise that most of the efforts of making a website accessible fall under visual accessibility. This group has a variety of alternate ways to access web pages; they might use a screen reader that reads the content of a page back to them. They might override the default styling on a website, allowing them to use colors that are higher contrast or fonts that are easier to read. They might change the scale of a website, increasing the font size until it's legible.

The blind are particularly impacted by an inaccessible web. A page might be structured in a way that's nonsensical if a user is using a screen reader. They might miss out on vital information in a graph or image. They might have to sit through listening to the navigation with every page load.

The goal of this section is to create a website that is accessible to a screen reader. A user should not lose any content or function simply because of the tool they are using.

Definition

Though there are many ways to determine complete blindness—from the legally blind who can't drive without glasses to the medically blind who have completely lost all sight—for the purposes of this book we define complete blindness as a user who is using a screen reader to access websites. Why not simply define it as those that have completely lost all their sight? Many people who have extremely little vision choose to use a screen reader. Screen readers are also popular for some people with extreme information processing disorders who have issues with reading text but not with the spoken word.

Annoyances, in Brief

The completely blind will almost always have issues with the following:

- Poorly structured HTML
- Images with no meaningful alt text
- Flash that is inaccessible
- Features that require vision, or where the fallback is poorly implemented
- Repetitive items that cannot be skipped
- Poorly structured forms

Screen Readers

Screen readers are specialized applications dedicated to reading aloud text on a screen. While every modern operating system comes with screen readers, a number of commercial applications have gained significant popularity. See Table 1-1 for a list of the most common screen readers.

Table 1-1. Common Screen Readers

Product	Operating System	Availability
JAWS	Windows	Commercial
VoiceOver	Mac	Included in System
Microsoft Narrator	Windows	Included in System
Orca	Unix	Bundled with Gnome
BRLTTY	Unix	Included with most Unix systems
ChromeVox	All OS's	An add-on developed by Google for Chrome

Since screen readers work by reading text that is visible on the screen or available through option tags, it's important to keep a few things in mind.

Things screen readers can do:

- Read all text visible on a page
- Read some tags that a sighted user will not be able to see (such as alt tags)
- List all headers and links

Things screen readers cannot do:

- Sometimes, read text based on your CSS layout
- Read text in images
- Detect navigation

It's also important to remember that, while modern screen readers have improved in the past few years, you might still have a user who is stuck using an older version. A new copy of JAWS—the most popular screen reader for Windows—costs over $800. A blind user might have issues purchasing it on her own, or might be in a place where she can't install it on her own, like a corporate office. Even if a newer version navigates around annoyances for you, resist the urge to not code for them anyway.

Creating Accessible Sites

HTML and Formatting

Logical flow

Since screen readers will read from the top of the page to the bottom, it's important that your document have a logical flow. With the rise of CSS, positioning has made it theoretically possible for the HTML flow of a page to have no resemblance to the end layout.

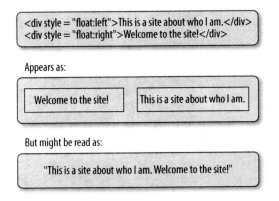

The problem with this is that, while some screen readers can work with the styled layout of a page, others may be working with the unstyled HTML to figure out what to read first. The safest way to structure your HTML is to have it flow in the same way you would structure it if it were being printed without formatting. Another way of thinking about this is how you would want your user's eye to travel over the page. This is the way you would want the page to be read.

If you don't want to start up your screen reader, try reading the unstyled HTML out loud. Does it still make sense?

Hiding text

Several of the following methods will deal with hiding text, so we should cover how to do that properly now.

Anyone who uses CSS will generally know about the visibility and display options. Setting visibility to hidden (or display to none) seems like the best way to remove text from a visual layout. There's one problem with this, though: screen readers often obey `display:none` and `visibility:hidden` by not reading out the hidden text. For instance, in Example 1-1, the header text wouldn't be read at all.

Example 1-1. Incorrect way of hiding text (nothing will be read)

In the CSS file:

```
h1 {
    background: url("welcome-image.png") no-repeat;
    height: 200px;
    width: 600px;
}

h1 span {
    display: none;
}
```

In the HTML file:

```
<h1><span>I will not be read.</span></h1>
```

A better alternative is to push the text off of the screen, as seen in Example 1-2.

Example 1-2. Hiding text properly

In your CSS file:

```
.hidden {
    text-indent: -5000px;
}
```

In your HTML:

```
<p class="hidden">This will be pushed off-screen</p>
```

Headers

Using headers is an important part of keeping the flow of your page sensible. Headers (`<h1>`, `<h2>`) should descend logically and should be used for section headers. It can be tempting to use headers for other uses, overriding them for decorative purposes. This breaks the structure of the document, and can be confusing to someone using a screen reader that announces that it has encountered a header.

Does this mean you should never replace a header with a graphic? Of course not. It's a common practice by designers to replace a header with a more stylized graphic. The text in the header should always match the text in the image, though. The decorative elements can be ignored. For example, if your header is on a sports site, and the designer has included a soccer ball on each header, you have to worry only about echoing the text. Make certain the proper way to hide text is used, pushing it off of the screen rather than using `display:none`.

Keep in mind that even if you decorate the header, it will still be read aloud through a screen reader. The text used in the header should remain informative to the user. Example 1-3 shows how headers might be read to a user using a screen reader.

Example 1-3. How headers are read by a screen reader

The following:

```
<h1>Astronomy News</h1>
<h2>New planet found!</h2>
<p>A new planet was found...</p>
```

might be read as:

```
"Heading level one, astronomy news. Heading level two, New planet found! A new planet was
found..."
```

Headers are also used by screen readers to help a user scan the document. It can read out all of the level one headers and allow the user to choose to skip to one. This way, a user can move quickly to the section that interests him most. How headers might be read out to a user who is scanning a page is shown in Example 1-4.

Example 1-4. Headers, as read when the user is scanning

The following:

```
<h1>Astronomy News</h1>
<h2>New planet found</h2>
<p>A new planet was found...</p>
<h1>Sports News</h1>
<h2>Preparations for the Winter Olympics Slowed</h2>
<p>Due to recent weather issues, preparations for the Olympics are...</p>
```

might be read as:

```
"Astronomy News. Sports News."
```

If headers are used incorrectly, however, the user's ability to jump around the document has been removed, and she must sit through the entire screen to find the content that interests her. Always make sure not to skip headers. If you've used `<h1>`, your next header should be `<h2>`, not `<h3>`.

Skipping navigation

Navigation, while necessary for moving around websites, is boring to listen to. A screen reader doesn't know to skip it, however, and every time a user loads a new page, the screen reader will read through the navigation again.

The simplest solution is to add an option to skip navigation that will be read only by a screen reader. If your page features local navigation, it should offer to skip to that as well. Sample code is shown in Example 1-5.

Example 1-5. Skip navigation

Above the navigation:

```
<span class="hidden">
    <a href = "#content">Skip to content</a>
</span>

<span class="hidden">
    <a href = "#pagenav">Skip to page navigation</a>
</span>
```

Before the page navigation:

```
<a name="pagenav"></a>
```

Before the content:

```
<a name="content"></a>
```

This way, the user will be able to skip to both the page's unique navigation or the page content every time a page loads.

Tables

Before the wide adoption of CSS, tables were often used for controlling layout. With even the most arcane of the common browsers now using CSS, tables no longer need to be used this way. Tables should be used only for tabular content, as screen readers may have problems navigating a page naturally.

If you have tabular data, such as a price list, sports scores, or a list of features, it absolutely should be put in a table rather than a series of divs. Screen readers treat tables differently, making it easier for a blind person to follow, as long as the tables are set up correctly.

Tables should always include scoping in their HTML. Scopes make it easier for the person listening to the screen reader to understand the values being read to them. Scopes indicate what type of data each column contains and what should be read out as a row. As the table is read aloud, the headers are spoken along with the row items, making it easier for a person using a screen reader to understand the data. Proper scoping is shown in Example 1-6, as well as how a scoped table is read to the user.

Example 1-6. Scoping Tables

This properly scoped table:

```
<table>
    <tr>
        <th scope="col">State</th>
```

```
        <th scope="col">Team name</th>
        <th scope="col">Mascot</th>
        <th scope="col">City</th>
    </tr>
    <tr>
        <th scope="row">District of Columbia</th>
        <td>Capitals</td>
        <td>Slapshot</td>
        <td>Washington</td>
    </tr>
    <tr>
        <th scope="row">Michigan</th>
        <td>Penguins</td>
        <td>Al the Octopus</td>
        <td>Detroit</td>
    </tr>
</table>
```

is read as:

```
"State: District of Columbia. Team name: Capitals. Mascot: Slapshot. City: Washington.
State: Michigan. Team name: Penguins. Mascot: Al the Octopus. City: Detroit."
```

Tables should also have a summary, giving a description of the data within it. If the table already has a caption, this should be used to elaborate on the contents, rather than repeat them. This way, the user can choose to listen through the table's contents or skip the table and move on to the next part of the content. Example 1-7 shows a proper summary and caption.

Example 1-7. Table with summary and caption

```
<table summary="A list of hockey teams, with their state, city, and mascot">
    <caption>NHL teams</caption>
        ...
</table>
```

Another use for the summary is to explicitly state generalizations about the contents of a table. A user without a screen reader might be able to glance over the data and draw conclusions about its contents. A user using a screen reader, however, would have to listen to every single data point and recall them all at the end to do the same thing. See Example 1-8 to see this in action.

Example 1-8. Table with summary stating generalizations

```
<table summary="A list of hockey tickets purchased every year, showing a general increase.">
    <synopsis>Ticket sales</synopsis>
        ...
</table>
```

Lastly, a user should be allowed to skip a table. No matter how vital a table might be to the content of a page, blind users shouldn't be forced to listen through them. Not every screen reader allows the user to skip tables, so some extra HTML might be required (shown in Example 1-9).

Example 1-9. Skipping a table

```
<p class="hidden"><a href = "#skiptable1">Skip a table about hockey teams and mascots</p>
<table>...</table>
<a name = "skiptable1" />
```

Images

Images do more than decorate a website; they convey information. This information cannot be lost simply because your user is using a screen reader.

If your image has any text in it, that text must be available to the screen reader. If you've styled a header, the easiest way to do this is to style the actual header tag, as shown in Example 1-10. This way, the screen reader knows that it's encountering a header and can announce this to the user.

Example 1-10. Replacing headers with images

In the CSS file:

```
h1#welcome {
    text-indent: -5000px;
    background: url("welcome-image.png") no-repeat;
    height: 300px;
}
```

In the HTML file:

```
<h1 id="welcome">Welcome</h1>
```

This is displayed as:

But will still be read as:

```
"Welcome"
```

For images with text that aren't a header, the text should be contained in the image's alt tag (Figure 1-1). This tag is read by the screen reader to the user, and should include not only the text in the image, but a description of what any of the images are as well.

```
<img src="dogs.png" alt="A number of dogs, showing their genetic diversity.">
```

The descriptions of the images shouldn't be limited to simple descriptions of what is in the picture. If there are certain elements of the image that are important, these should

Figure 1-1. Using alt tags

be spelled out. Why was the image included for a sighted user? Was there something significant in the image that adds to the content of the page?

It's not uncommon for images to have captions, but the urge to simply make the caption the alt text should be resisted. While, technically, 508 compliance would be satisfied, the user is no better off. What they'll end up hearing is the caption twice, which does nothing to explain the importance of the image. If the caption does nothing to add to the image, perhaps it's worth wondering if the caption is needed at all. Figure 1-2 shows an image with a caption that adds to the alt text rather than repeating it.

```
<div>
    <img src = "galaxy.png" alt = "Two galaxies are shown close together. The arms of
one of the galaxies are long and thin." />
    <div class = "caption">The results of two galaxies colliding</div>
</div>
```

This will be read as:

```
"Image: Two galaxies are shown close together. The arms of one of the galaxies are long
and thin. The results of two galaxies colliding."
```

There are exceptions to the alt text rule. There are many instances when an image does not add to the content of the page, but is being used for branding or layout. If a designer

The results of two galaxies colliding

Figure 1-2. Good captioning

has had to use a spacer image, that image should have no alt text at all, allowing the screen reader to pass over it silently. The same goes for styled list bullets or branding.

If a logo is presented several times in a page, the first can certainly have alt text. Beyond that, however, any further alt text becomes tiresome. In general, if you wouldn't want to read it aloud to a colleague, the image should be skipped in order to maintain flow and avoid annoying the user.

Keep in mind that not including alt text will cause automated programs to falsely report that image. This is one of the reasons why good 508 testing is done both automatically and manually. Be prepared to justify why that image does not need alt text, and in the case of spacer or decorative images, see if there's a way to remove the image and instead use CSS.

Graphs and diagrams

Graphs, while still images, require a special amount of consideration. In this case, if every data point and bit of text were read out, the graph would be useless. With graphs, the rule of reading out all text can be bent in favor of giving an overall feel for the content of the graph.

Some good rules of thumb for creating alt text for a graph:

- If the graph image has a title in it, make certain to include that title.
- State what is being charted (e.g., what variable against what constant, or what percentages of a population).
- If there is a caption for the graph, take care not to repeat its content in the alt text.
- State the trends in the graph as plainly as possible, but refrain from drawing conclusions (e.g., "The drop in sales proves that the new product was a bust.")
- If two data points are being graphed against each other then the variable is being graphed against the constant. In other words, the thing being graphed on the Y-axis is being graphed against the X-axis. Make certain the alt text reflects that.

A quick test for a well-described chart is to show the alt text to another person, then show them the chart. Do the trends you described match with the chart, or did you accidentally miss something? Figure 1-3 shows a properly captioned chart.

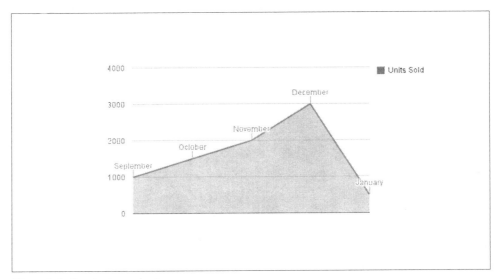

Figure 1-3. Captioning a chart

```
<div>
    <img
        src = "christmas.png"
        alt = "A chart titled Christmas Sales, with units sold being graphed against
the months September through January. Sales start at a thousand units in September,
double to two thousand in November, rise again to three thousand in December. In
January, the sales drop down to five hundred."
    />
    <div class = "caption">Sales diving after Christmas</div>
</div>
```

Forms

If your website has forms (and most do, even if it's simply a search field), special consideration is need to make these usable to a screen reader. It can be easy to get lost within a form when it's laid out poorly.

Labels. Labels are extremely important to screen readers, as they determine what fields go with what form fields, and determine how a user should navigate through the form. Fortunately, they're also easy to make accessible. Titles and labels should always match each other, so when the screen reader processes the page, the screen reader can read the text within the label and also announce the kind of form field the user will be working with (see Example 1-11).

Example 1-11. Labels in forms

```
<label for="last">Last Name: </label>
<input type="text" name="lastname" id="last">
```

The only form fields that don't require labels are buttons, since these already contain the text that explains what they are. Make certain that this text is helpful, however. If the button has been styled with a graphic, make certain the text in the graphic matches the text in the value attribute (Figure 1-4).

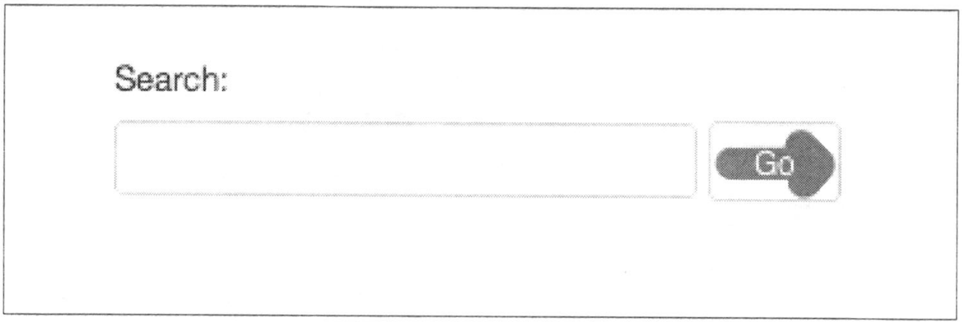

Figure 1-4. Correct labeling for a submit button

```
<label for="search">Search: </label>
<input type="text" name="search" id="search">
<input type="submit" value="Go">
```

Errors. If your site includes a form that validates itself, make certain that if the form encounters errors, it errors out vocally. Rather than simply making the incorrect field turn red (a common design choice), add text that explains which part of the form is incorrect, and why (Figure 1-5).

```
<p class = "error">That's not a email address. Email addresses should have the format
of user@host.com</p>
<label for="email">Email: </label>
<input type="text" name="email" id="email">
<input type="submit" value="Go">
```

Name

Mary Beth

Email

badinput   That is not a valid email address.

Save changes   Cancel

Figure 1-5. Erroring out vocally

This actually increases the usability of the form overall, since many users would like to know exactly what they need to do to get the form to submit, rather than guess at what might work.

CAPTCHA and challenge responses. Often, forms that allow an anonymous person to submit them will include a form element intended to deter bots from spamming the website. The most typical of these is CAPTCHA ("Completely Automated Public Turing test to tell Computers and Humans Apart"), which asks a user to type in letters or words from an image. Some samples of popular formats for CAPTCHAs are shown in Figure 1-6.

A CAPTCHA, of course, is a huge issue for someone using a screen reader, since the letters cannot be included in the alt text. If they were, the test would be rendered useless, allowing for bots to simply read that text and enter it.

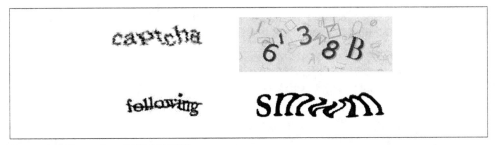

Figure 1-6. Examples of CAPTCHAS

One work-around is to offer an audio CAPTCHA as well. A user using a screen reader could play the audio of a voice saying the numbers and letters, and then enter them into the form. CAPTCHA.net offers a widget that gives both a visual and an audio option. If the user is using a text-only browser, however, he wouldn't be able to use the form at all (as seen in Figure 1-7).

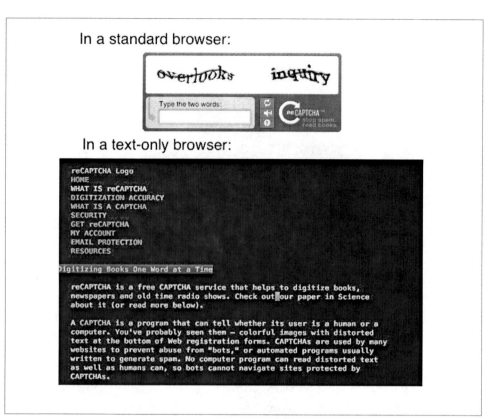

Figure 1-7. CAPTCHA in a text browser versus a typical browser

If the CAPTCHA can't be used at all, make certain that a user has a way to submit information, even if it's offering an email address or an alternate form that doesn't use CAPTCHA.

If your site chooses to use CAPTCHA that has an audio fallback, make certain to text the fallback rigorously. Just like the images used for CAPTCHA, it can be easy for the text to become too garbled to be used.

Another option for a challenge response is to use a question that a human would find easy to answer but a robot would not. For example, a user could be asked what sport uses a hockey puck. To a human, that's a fairly simple question to answer (the answer is in the question, after all). A robot would have trouble parsing it, unless it was rather sophisticated. Care must be taken, though, that the answer would be obvious to any user, in spite of cultural lines (for example, a website created by a South American developer might find it quite intuitive that the country west of Brazil is Peru, but North American users might be stumped). One example that can cross cultural lines is in Figure 1-8.

Figure 1-8. An alternative question to CAPTCHA

Questions such as these should be regularly rotated, since it is still possible to find a way to crack them after a human sees them.

While writing questions, keep in mind the portion of the website's audience that might be completely blind. The question about the color of a Pepsi label may seem obvious, but might be unanswerable by a blind person who hasn't bothered to remember that Pepsi usually uses blue.

One last option is a test that is actually invisible to sighted users: the honeypot, shown in Figure 1-9. A form field is added to the site, then hidden. A bot would automatically fill in all fields, so if that field is filled in, that user must be a bot. The form fails silently, not alerting the bot that something has gone awry.

Name:

Comment: Submit

Figure 1-9. A form with a honeypot

```
<form>
    <label for='name'>Name:</label><input id='name' type='text' />
    <label class='hide' for='state'>Please leave this blank</label><input class='hide'
id='state' type = 'text' />
    <label for='comment'>Comment:</label><input id='comment' type='text' />
    <input value='Submit' type='submit' />
</form>
```

While effective, a user using a screen reader must be told to skip the honeypot portion of the form. If he fills it out, and the form fails, he wouldn't know that anything had gone wrong. If the form fails vocally, a bot would be alerted that one of the fields is a honeypot, and it would be able to try again, but this time knowing to leave a section of the form blank.

Another version of the honeypot is where all users can see the form field, but it's obvious to a human that it shouldn't be filled out, or a different answer should be selected. Figure 1-10 shows a visual honeypot, where the answer the person should pick is obvious.

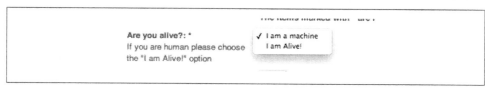

Figure 1-10. A form with a visible honeypot

Whatever method fits a website, the end goal should always be to ensure that all users not only can use it, but that they are not overly annoyed by it.

JavaScript

A common myth regarding screen readers is that they're incapable of processing JavaScript, so any site that uses JavaScript is automatically inaccessible. Screen readers have come a long way since the early 2000s, and most have no issues with JavaScript. According to a 2011 survey by *WebAIM.org*, 98.4% of respondents had JavaScript enabled. Most of the remaining 1.6% were using browsers that support AdBlock, so it is possible that they had AdBlock installed, which would make it impossible to detect JavaScript.

This doesn't mean, however, that JavaScript is automatically accessible. Care must still be taken to ensure that users using screen readers can access the functions and content of a website, just as a sighted user might.

Keep in mind, though, that JavaScript is still unusable by pure text browsers, which may render your site unusable. At the very least, make certain that the site functions with JavaScript turned off. This would also help those who are in a corporate or public environment, where JavaScript is sometimes turned off on shared terminals. Not every mobile browser supports JavaScript, or supports it in awkward ways.

The safest way to add JavaScript to a website is to start with a site that works without it at all. All of the functionality and content should be present, even if the presentation isn't as slick as the designer might have liked. This way, if a user doesn't have JavaScript, she has something to fall back on.

Now that there's a baseline, the developer can begin to add a scripting layer. This scripting layer should remain separate from the content, as shown in Example 1-12. In other words, no inline JavaScript, please.

Why, in Example 1-12, is one example good and one bad? One only needs to look at the HTML. If the user has no JavaScript, the first code sample wouldn't work at all. With the second, the user would simply go to a new page, where the survey could be taken, rather than having a new window opened.

Example 1-12. Inline versus external JavaScript

Inline (bad):

```
<a href = "Javascript:window.open('survey.html')">Take our survey!</a>
```

External (good)

In the HTML file:

```
<a href = "survey.html" id="new_window">Take out survey!</a>
```

In the JavaScript file:

```
function doNewWindow() {
    if (document.getElementsByTagName) {
        var links = document.getElementsByTagName("a");
        for (var i = 0; i < links.length; i++) {
            if (links[i].className.match("new_window")) {
                links[i].onclick = function () {
                    window.open(this.getAttribute("href"));
                    return false;
                };
            }
        }
    }
}
```

Frames and iframes

Frames and iframes, while readable to almost every screen reader, can be disorienting if not set up correctly. The user should always be able to tell where they are on a page, move around easily, and have an alternative if they cannot, or choose not, to use frames.

Frames. If at all possible, avoid the use of frames. Not only are they more difficult for screen readers to cope with, but even sighted users report issues using them. Sometimes, however, redesigning a website to not use frames isn't possible, especially if they're built on a framework that uses them heavily.

In this instance, keep in mind that a screen reader doesn't allow for scanning the same way a browser allows a sighted person to scan a web page. It starts at the beginning of the page and reads in the order that seems to make the most sense. If a website uses frames, a screen reader will begin reading at the first frame, read through it completely, then move to the next frame. A user, however, can hear a list of available frames and skip among them as needed.

The frames shouldn't be given generic titles such as "frame1," "frame2," or "frame3." These names don't give the user any indication of what is actually contained in the frames. Better names would be "navigation," "content," and "related content." Frames with useful titles are shown in Example 1-13.

Example 1-13. Frames with titles

```
<!DOCTYPE HTML PUBLIC "-//W3C//DTD HTML 4.01 Frameset//EN" "http://www.w3.org/TR/html4/
frameset.dtd">
<frameset>
    <frame src="menu.html" title="Navigation" name="nav" />
    <frame src="content1.html" title="Content" name="content" />
    <frame src="related.html" title="Related content" name="related" />
</frameset>
```

Also, if the user is not using frames (or can't see them), they should be given an option to go to a page without frames.

Iframes. Iframes are reportedly much better supported by screen readers, but steps still have to be taken to make certain that they're accessible for a screen reader.

As usual, accessibility comes with well-formed HTML. The frameset should be properly declared, rather than hoping the browser will sort out what it's supposed to display. Example 1-14 shows a properly declared frameset.

Example 1-14. Iframe DOCTYPE

```
<!DOCTYPE HTML PUBLIC "-//W3C//DTD HTML 4.01 Frameset//EN" "http://www.w3.org/TR/html4/
frameset.dtd">
```

Each frame should also have its own title attribute that describes the content of the frame. It can be tempting for a web developer to refer to the frames by their position, especially if she's using a content management system or framework, where data might change dynamically. However, this leads to confusion for someone using a screen reader when the user is trying to scan the page. A description of "middle frame" doesn't help the user navigate the page quickly.

Also, some screen readers will read out the name of the HTML page linked in the iframe. Though this is rare, developers should try to name the files something sensible, like "menu.html" or "instructions.html."

If the user is using a screen reader that cannot handle frames, he'll be dependent on the developer providing noframes content. A common solution for those who can't use frames or iframes is to include code similar to that in Example 1-15. The only text displayed to a user who can't use frames is a suggestion that he use a browser that can cope with frames.

Example 1-15. Bad alternate content for iframes

```
<iframe src = "menu.html">We're sorry, this site requires frames.</iframe>
```

In Example 1-15, the user is given no clue as to what the content might have been, or how to get to it. A slightly better option is to offer the user a link to the missing content, as seen in Example 1-16.

Example 1-16. Linking to frame content

```
<iframe src = "menu.html">
    <a href = "menu.html" title = "Menu">Our menu</a>
</iframe>
```

Often, though, HTML pages for iframes are bare-bones, stripped of navigation and any other global site features. The best option, shown in Example 1-17, is to offer a page that is as fully featured as any other page within the website.

Example 1-17. Linking to alternate page

```
<iframe src = "menu.html">
    <a href = "menu_noframe.html" title="Menu">Our menu</a>
</iframe>
```

This is the least jarring to a user that can't use iframes and is on a screen reader. Her user experience isn't suddenly changed, and the fact that she can't use frames or iframes isn't being unnecessarily harangued upon.

Flash

Flash is often criminalized as being completely inaccessible. Like JavaScript, it's unfair to judge Flash out of hand. Flash can be very accessible, as long as the browser is compliant, and in fact, can be even more accessible to some groups, as will be seen in later chapters.

The largest problem with making Flash accessible isn't the tool itself, but the fact that some developers don't use the tools provided by Adobe or other open source tools. A 2009 survey of screen readers found that 34% of users found Flash objects very difficult to use, and 37% found them somewhat difficult to use. This was in spite of accessibility tools being built into most products since 2001.

Just because something can be made in Flash, however, doesn't always mean it should.

The first step to having an accessible Flash object on a page is determining if it would be better to provide an alternative page for screen readers. For example, if the Flash object is a slide presentation, perhaps the content can simply be offered on another page in a plainer format (see Figure 1-11). The user will likely not care about the slide transitions and the pauses while they execute might be annoying.

One place to avoid Flash is in the navigation. Not only should navigation remain unobtrusive for basic usability principles, but if the user doesn't have Flash, he might not be able to use the site at all! Instead, use CSS and JavaScript to create attractive navigation elements, leaving Flash for more complicated features.

Flash objects, if they're intended to be accessed by the blind, should be accessible by the keyboard, so the user can tab through them, and pressing Enter should count the same as a click from a mouse.

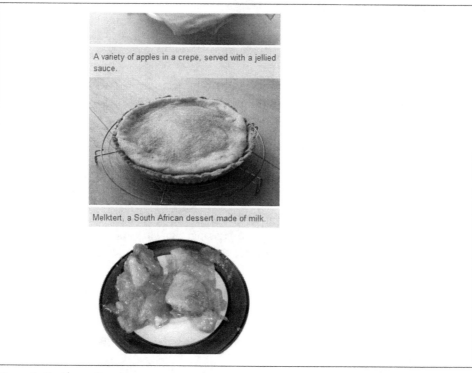

A variety of apples in a crepe, served with a jellied sauce.

Melktert, a South African dessert made of milk.

Figure 1-11. Alternative page

The Flash object should not automatically play audio, as that could interfere with the screen reader's reading of the page content. Two voices overlaying would be extremely frustrating to a blind user. Auto-play is a bad idea for any user, in fact, so disabling it should be a priority on any site. A common complaint is that advertisers will sometimes include videos that auto-play, and are out of the control of the site. How valuable is an advertiser who drives away a website's users, though?

The Flash object should have text cues for the screen reader so the user will know how to navigate. Any instructions for special keys should be spelled out for the user as soon as she hits the Flash object, so she can start using it immediately. For example, in Figure 1-12, the user has come upon a slide show. Before reading the text of the slides, the user should be instructed on how to move to the next slide, move back to the previous slide, reread the current slide, or hear a list of slide titles.

Lastly, consider whether the Flash object needs to be made in Flash at all. With the slides in Figure 1-12, a stunning version could be made out of HTML5, CSS, and Java-Script without needing an extra plug-in to use. Many workplaces and schools block Flash, and some browsers, such as Lynx, cannot work with it at all.

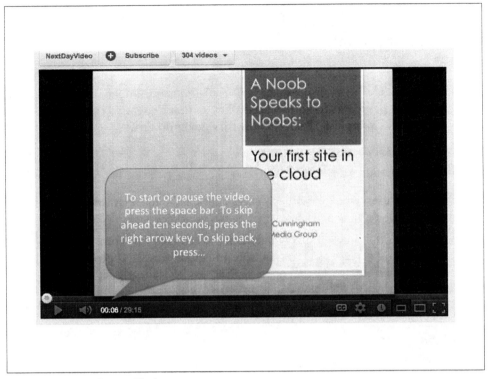

Figure 1-12. Text Cues in Flash

Many developers worry that every Flash application needs to be accessible, but there are exceptions. For instance, a Flash arcade game would be impossible to build for a blind person. Don't rush to conclude that your Flash application doesn't need to be compliant at all, though. Each group has their own issues with Flash, which we will cover in other sections.

Access keys

Access keys are a tool that allows a user, by hitting certain key combinations, to easily move to certain elements on a web page, or go to set pages within a website. Almost all modern browsers support access keys (see Table 1-2).

Table 1-2. Browsers that support access keys

Browser	OS	Version
Chrome	Mac, Windows, Linux	3+
Firefox	Mac, Windows, Linux	2+
Internet Explorer	Windows	8+
Safari	Mac, Windows	3+

Browser	OS	Version
Opera	Mac, Windows, Linux	All
Konqueror	Mac, Windows, Linux	All

An access key is added to a website by adding an attribute to an anchor tag. For example, let's say a developer wants to add an access key so that a user can easily move to the next blog article. Example 1-18 shows how they might do this.

Example 1-18. Adding an access key to a page

```
<a href = 'daytwo.html' accesskey='n'>Next</a>
```

Now, when the user uses "n" with his access keys, he'll automatically be sent to the next page.

At the moment, the only official standard for access keys is from the UK, though international standards are emerging as more and more sites are choosing to use access keys, or are using frameworks that come with access keys already set up, like Plone or vBulletin. See Table 1-3 for some common access keys.

Table 1-3. Common access keys

Key	Action
1	Home Page
2	Skip to content
3	Site Map
4	Search field focus
5	Advanced Search
6	Site navigation tree
9	Contact information
0	Access Key details

As a side note, another popular convention is to assign the numbers to the navigation items on the global navigation, with one being the first item, and zero being the last. Why is zero last? The order has less to do with the numbers' numerical order, and more to do with their order on the keyboard. Most keyboards list zero at the end of the numbers row, so that's the order that's used for navigation items.

If you wanted to make your main navigation accessible with access keys, it might end up looking like the code in Example 1-19.

Example 1-19. A main menu with access keys

```
<ul>
    <li><a href = "/" accesskey = "H">Home</a></li>
```

```
    <li><a href = "/products/" accesskey='1'>Products</a></li>
    <li><a href = "/store/" accesskey='2'>Store</a></li>
    <li><a href = "/contact-us/" accesskey='3'>Contact Us</a>
</ul>
```

Note how the first navigation item is set to H, rather than a number. This is a stylistic choice, since that could just as easily have been set to 1. What isn't a stylistic choice is the order of the numbers. To many developers, 0 comes before 1. In this case, however, 0 is the last element in the series. If your navigation has more than 10 elements (or 11, including home), this may be a good time to consider making the top level of the site narrower.

WAI-ARIA

One of the most recent developments in accessibility is the acceptance of WAI-ARIA (Web Accessibility Initiative-Accessible Rich Internet Applications) into the W3C standards. Created specifically for rich Internet applications, WAI-ARIA allows disabled users to interact with even the most complex of applications by declaring certain elements on the page to have a specific role.

WAI-ARIA works by adding meta-data to an application's HTML tags. Figure 1-13 shows how roles can be added to a drag and drop feature to make it accessible. Normally, the user would have to use a mouse to drag an item from the "Available Fruit" section to the "Basket." With ARIA enabled, a user who can't use the mouse can move the items around by tabbing to them, hitting enter, then moving to where they want the item to be.

```
<div id="dragdrop" role="application">
    <h2 id="available">Available produce</h2>
    <ul id="available_list">
        <li class="draggable" role="button">Apple</li>
        <li class="draggable" role="button">Banana</li>
        <li class="draggable" role="button">Mango</li>
        <li class="draggable" role="button">Papaya</li>
        <li class="draggable" role="button">Kiwi</li>
        <li class="draggable" role="button">Pear</li>
    </ul>

    <h2 id="basket">Basket</h2>
    <ul id="basket_list">
        <li class="empty">None</li>
    </ul>
</div>
```

While a developer can make her own JavaScript for ARIA-enabled applications, it's worth noting that many frameworks already have ARIA built in, either fully or for specific widgets. YUI, Google Web Toolkit, and jQuery are several that either include or are planning to include WAI-ARIA.

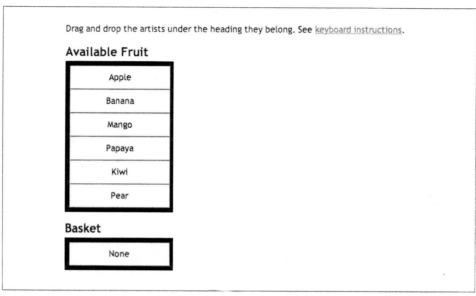

Drag and drop the artists under the heading they belong. See keyboard instructions.

Available Fruit

Apple
Banana
Mango
Papaya
Kiwi
Pear

Basket

None

Figure 1-13. ARIA example

A full introduction to ARIA would be a book in itself, so this section will be only an introduction to some of the things ARIA can do.

Alerts for updates

A particularly sticky issue for screen readers is websites that update without reloading the page. Many sites will include live feeds or post alerts. These updates might be of vital importance to the user (for example, a bank warning that the user is about to be timed out) or might be of little consequence (like a Twitter widget that updates automatically).

WAI-ARIA includes several items that alert the screen reader that something has changed and suggests how urgent the update is. The status role can be added to a container that can be updated, as shown in Example 1-20. It can be set to "polite" or "assertive." "Polite" will interrupt as soon as the screen reader is done with whatever task it's executing (usually reading a block of text), whereas "assertive" will read out the update to the user immediately.

Example 1-20. The status role

```
<p role="status" aria-life="assertive">You will be logged out in thirty seconds.</p>
```

alert and alertdialog, shown in Example 1-21, can be added as a role to a div that has just been updated and can take input from the user. Alerts are assumed to be assertive, but can be set to be passive as well.

Example 1-21. The alertdialog role

```
<!-- From http://test.cita.uiuc.edu/aria/alertdialog/alertdialog1.php -->

<div role="application">

    <div id="guess1" class="guess">

      <h2>Number Guessing Game</h2>

      <p class="input">
        <label id="guess1_label" for="guess1_text">Guess a number between 1 and 10</label>
        <input type="text" id="guess1_text" size="3" aria-labelledby="guess1_label" aria-
invalid="false">
      </p>

      <p class="input">
        <input class="button" id="guess1_check" type="button" value="Check My Guess">
        <input class="button" id="guess1_again" type="button" value="Play Again">
      </p>
      <div id="alert1" role="alertdialog" tabindex="-1" aria-hidden="true" aria-
labelledby="alert1_title"><p id="alert1_title" class="title">Alert Box</p><p
id="alert1_message">No Message</p><input id="alert1_close" type="button" value="Close"></
div></div>
</div>
```

A `marquee` is a live section that includes information that's expected to update quite often, but is considered non-essential. Stock tickers, latest news widgets, and Twitter feeds are common examples of items often included on a website that have little bearing to the main content of the page. Marquees are set to not update the user at all by default.

Navigation

The `navigation` role can be used to designate something as a landmark for a navigation. A page can have several of these, allowing the user to move around them with ease. To declare something as navigation, simply give the containing element the role of `navigation` (see Example 1-22).

Example 1-22. The navigation role

```
<ul id="navigation2" role="navigation" aria-labelledby="nav2_label">
  <li class="nobullet"><a href="http://www.uiuc.edu/">undergrads</a></li>
  <li><a href="http://www.uiuc.edu/">Graduates</a></li>
  <li><a href="http://www.uiuc.edu/">Parents</a></li>
  <li><a href="http://www.uiuc.edu/">Alumni</a></li>
  <li><a href="http://www.uiuc.edu/">Faculty / Staff</a></li>
  <li><a href="http://www.uiuc.edu/">Employers</a></li>
</ul>
```

The `navigation` role doesn't require any JavaScript to work. Screen readers will note them and announce them to the user.

Often a navigation will have drop-down elements. In this case, it's useful to give these elements a `tree` or `treegrid` role. This indicates that the element has child elements that can be expanded or contracted.

Other semantic markup

Web applications often include menus. Giving these items a `menu` or `menubar` role makes them easier for a screen reader to find and use. Figure 1-14 shows how a menu might be made ARIA-friendly.

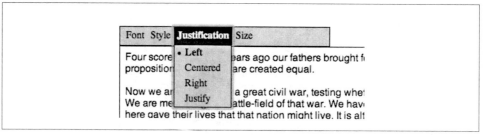

Figure 1-14. Example of a menu with ARIA

```
<ul id="mb1" class="menubar" role="menubar" title="Styling Menu" aria-controls="st1">
  <li id="mb1_menu1" role="menuitem" tabindex="0" aria-haspopup="true" class="">
  Font
    <ul id="fontMenu" class="menu" role="menu" aria-hidden="true" style="display:
none; ">
      <li id="sans-serif" role="menuitemradio" tabindex="-1" aria-controls="st1" aria-
checked="true" class="checked">
        Sans-serif
      </li>
      <li id="serif" role="menuitemradio" tabindex="-1" aria-controls="st1" aria-
checked="false">
        Serif
      </li>
      <li id="monospace" role="menuitemradio" tabindex="-1" aria-controls="st1" aria-
checked="false">
        Monospace
      </li>
      <li id="fantasy" role="menuitemradio" tabindex="-1" aria-controls="st1" aria-
checked="false">
        Fantasy
      </li>
    </ul>
    ...
</ul>
```

Another common tool on interactive websites is a timer, whether used for a game or for forms that are set to time out. WAI-ARIA includes a `timer` role that allows the developer to indicate that something is either counting down from or up to a set point in time. By default, timers don't announce their changes to the user, but this can be overridden by the developer. If the developer does override it, however, he should take care not to be too overzealous; the user probably doesn't need the seconds read out whenever the screen reader isn't busy.

Resources

As stated before, this is but a small sample of the items contained in the WAI-ARIA specifications. As more libraries have adopted the standard, more resources have been created. More resources are in Table 1-4.

Table 1-4. WAI-ARIA resources

Website	URL	Description
Official WAI-ARIA documentation	http://www.w3.org/TR/wai-aria/	The technical documentation for WAI-ARIA
Mozilla's ARIA documentation	https://developer.mozilla.org/en/Accessibility/ARIA/	Mozilla's documentation on how to use ARIA. Includes examples for almost every role.
Yahoo! Accessibility	http://yaccessibilityblog.com/library/tag/aria/	Blog posts on developing with ARIA
Opera's Introduction to WAI-ARIA	http://dev.opera.com/articles/view/introduction-to-wai-aria/	Multilingual introduction to WAI-ARIA
The Paciello Group's ARIA blog entries	http://www.paciellogroup.com/blog/category/wai-aria/	Discussion about the uses for ARAI, as well as future development

Testing

Since nearly all operating systems come with their own screen readers, technically, you already have the tools to test your website. Using a screen reader takes practice, however, and can be impractical for testing existing sites in a timely manner.

Automated testing

A wealth of automated testing tools exist that can test an entire site. They come in all flavors, from free to the enterprise, as well as those that run as web applications to ones that you host locally. Which one you choose will come down to your needs and budget. See Table 1-5 for some common automated testing tools.

Table 1-5. Common automated testing tools

Tool	Description	Approximate cost
Cynthia Says	Web-based	Free
WAVE	Web-based	Free
Compliance Sheriff	Desktop	Varies
Rational Rose	Server- and desktop-based	Varies

There are severe limits to automated testing, though. For one, automated tests can't make judgment calls. While we know that spacer images should never be given alt text, almost every automated tool out there that sees images without alt text will fail the site. They also might fail to see that when you styled a header with an image containing text, you failed to match the text the screen reader would read and the text a browser would display. An automated tool will probably not pick up that a content editor copied the captions for images into the alt text.

Another thing an automated tool will often not be able to do is judge the flow of your content. Most will note that you're using headers, but not have any issues if you're not using them correctly (for instance, styling a header to be a section divider). This is something that someone will have to experience firsthand to determine if the page is truly friendly to a screen reader.

Manual testing

As useful as automated testing is, it can't give you the whole picture of what your site is like for a person using a screen reader. Using a screen reader can take quite a bit of practice, but there are some workarounds. One, a Firefox add-on called Fangs will render any page as it might be seen by a screen reader. The text, rather than the spoken word, is given to the tester, allowing her to read through the data to see if the order is still logical, and to ensure that all data is being represented.

One thing the Fangs cannot do is test more complex applications, like a video player. For this, a tester would want to actually use a screen reader. Screen readers can feel very alien to a user who's used to using his eyes to seek out information, rather than using sound and key strokes. The idea here, though, isn't to be as fast as a daily user. The idea is to make sure that more intricate functionality is in tact for people using a screen reader.

Screen readers are different for every OS, but they do follow some basic principles, so testing in every screen reader will probably not be necessary. In general, all screen readers:

- List out headers for the user
- Read alt tags for images
- List links on a page
- Use access keys
- Read out tables in the column:content format
- Will not read out `display:none` or `visibility:hidden`

Covering the above points, at a minimum, will still make a site much more usable by a blind user.

CHAPTER 2

Visual Accessibility—Other Types

Visual accessibility isn't limited to just the blind. Those with low vision or color blindness can also have issues when it comes to using websites. Navigation may disappear if the user makes the font large enough to read or vital diagrams might appear muddled and ambiguous if he can't tell certain colors apart.

Low Vision

For the purposes of this book, a user with low vision is classified as anyone who must adjust the settings for the monitor to use a computer but is not using a screen reader. They might use a screen magnifier, or they might adjust the font size for a website. They also might override a site's default fonts and colors in favor of ones that are higher contrast. These users might be people who are losing their vision, or they might be people who simply forgot their reading glasses.

Annoyances

Those that have low vision will often have issues with the following:

- Sites that lose functionality or content when the font size is changed
- Colors that don't contrast highly enough
- Sites where default styles can't be overridden
- Text in images
- Confusing forms

Grow Gracefully

With modern browsers, one of the most common ways to make a website easier to read is to increase the font size. With proper CSS, this should cause the entire site to grow as well, including layout, images, embedded objects, and navigation. Though certain images may look best at certain dimensions, they might be impossible for a user to see, which would defeat the purpose of including the image. Figure 2-1 shows an instance of a navigation not growing gracefully, leaving some of the text obscured.

Figure 2-1. Not growing gracefully

To test if your site grows gracefully, simply open it in a browser and increase the font. Usually, this is done by pressing CTRL++ (⌘-+). Things to watch for:

- Are all navigation elements still visible?
- Is everything staying on approximately the same line as before, or are elements being forced into a narrow column?
- Are images growing as well as the text?
- Are embedded objects, such as Flash objects, growing along with the rest of the site?

It is also important to test all browsers for graceful growth. Not every browser deals with growth in the same ways, just as not every browser deals with CSS in the same ways.

Contrast

No matter how gracefully a design grows, it cannot combat a color selection that is muddled and difficult to read. Wherever text is used, the contrast between the background and the foreground should be as high as possible. The best contrast for almost everyone, surprisingly, isn't pure black against pure white. The most readable is off-black against off-white, as shown in Figures 2-2 and 2-3.

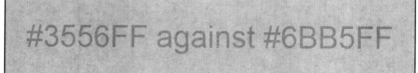

Figure 2-2. An example of good contrast

```
#222222 against #FFFFEE
```

Figure 2-3. An example of bad contrast

Though limiting for a designer, content should always feature optimal contrasts, no matter how boring they may seem. This decision benefits everyone, as reading for extended periods on a poor site with poor contrast can cause eye strain and headaches, eventually driving users away.

Overrides

Though less common these days, a design should also never block a user from using her own stylesheet. In the early days of the Internet, when impossible color combinations were more common, many people chose to force their browser to use their own stylesheets. Backgrounds, foregrounds, and link colors were set to user-defined defaults, no matter what site they were on.

How could a user be blocked from using their own styles? If too much of a site's content is locked into Flash or images, a low-vision user won't be able to use color and font combinations that work for them. Many users also use add-ons, like GreaseMonkey, to make websites easier to read (amongst other non-usability related reasons). Blocking add-ons like GreaseMonkey can hurt users who rely on it to use websites comfortably.

Forms

Forms can also be difficult to those with low vision. Cursors, no matter how much a page has been zoomed in, can be difficult to track. A simple solution is to add styling to forms, so that when a field has focus, it is highlighted. Figure 2-4 shows a form with focus indication styled.

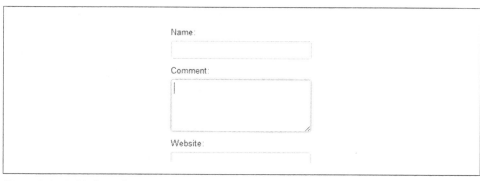

Figure 2-4. Highlight on focus

This way, a user can easily tell where he is in the form, and doesn't accidentally start to enter text in incorrectly. This is also a boon to users with normal vision, who might become lost on larger forms.

Color Blindness

Color blindness affects approximately 5% of the US population[1], and ranges from mild cases like telling certain reds apart, to those who can see no color at all. How does this impact those trying to use a website? Though many think only of how text is displayed, a great amount of information is stored within items that are dependent on color. Many navigations, stylish though they may be, couch their text in colors that may be invisible to certain segments of the population. Visual indicators have become ubiquitous, but are often useless to people with certain kinds of color blindness (see Table 2-1).

Table 2-1. Types of color blindness

Type	Colors that appear similar	% of population affected
Protanopia	Red and green. Some colors may appear more intense than they would appear to someone with normal vision.	1% of all males
Deuteranopia	Red and green, but colors retain proper intensity.	1% of all males
Tritanopia	Blue and yellow.	Less than 1% of population
Complete chromatopsia	All colors are affected. Users see only shades of gray. Also, users often have poor vision as well.	1 in 30,000 people
Incomplete chromatopsia	All colors are affected. Users see colors dimly. Also, users often have poor vision as well.	1 in 30,000 people
Protanomaly	Reds are less intense and can appear black.	1% of males, 0.01% of females

1. U.S. statistics are used throughout this chapter. Collecting statistics on a global basis are difficult, since some cultures don't collect data on it, others have high prevalence, and others have extremely low prevalence.

Type	Colors that appear similar	% of population affected
Deuteranomaly	Greens are muted.	6% of males, 0.4% of females
Tritanomaly	Blue and yellow.	0.01% of the population

Color blindness not only prevents the user from seeing certain colors, but can alter how two colors contrast each other (Figure 2-5). Red and green, to those with normal vision, have strong contrast, but to someone with red-green color blindness, the two appear very similar. Also, the contrasts aren't constant between different kinds of color blindness. A set of colors with wonderful contrast to a person with red-green color blindness may be muddled to someone with yellow-blue color blindness.

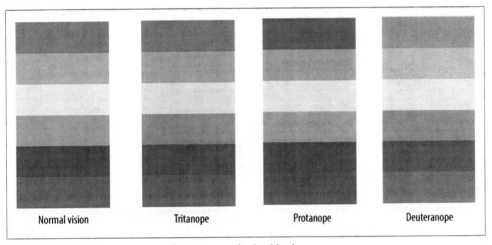

Figure 2-5. Visible spectrum to different types of color blindness

Another pitfall of designing for color blindness is the use of images where colors are used to convey important information. Perhaps a website has an image of a subway map and refers to the "green line." How would someone who can't tell green from red tell which line is which? Another pitfall often comes with scientific images. A cell with its parts color-coded in yellow and blue would be impossible for some people to decipher.

Annoyances in Brief

The color blind often have issues with the following items:

- Color schemes that aren't high enough contrast
- Figures without keys for color coding
- Figures that are confusing due to swapped intensity
- Images with poor contrast

Optimization of Color Schemes

Ideally, the best time to optimize your site for color blindness is at the beginning, before designs have been set in stone. That way, design colors and accessibility can marry in a way that pleases everyone.

Because there are so many different kinds of color blindness, it's often best to leave color scheme optimization to already existing tools. Happily, many have already been created that not only work as a web application, but that also plug in to tools you may already be using (see Table 2-2).

In essence, each tool will work very similarly: once you've selected a color palette, you can preview how it will look to each of the different types. The goal should be an attractive palette that retains its high contrast through each of the subtypes.

Table 2-2. Tools for testing color schemes

Tool	Operating System	Cost
Color Scheme Designer	All (web application)	Free
Sim Daltonism	Mac OS	Free
Color Vision	All (web application)	Free
Adobe Photoshop (as of CS5)	Windows / Mac	Approximately $600

Once a color scheme has been generated, a designer can then create a mock up of the website to put the scheme through its paces. Plug-ins exist for almost every popular design tool, once again allowing a designer to preview a design to ensure that colors that become muddled aren't placed too close to each other.

If a site has already been created and a tester wishes to see it in through the eyes of various types of color blindness, plug-ins also exist for many web browsers (see Table 2-3).

Table 2-3. Tools for colors on existing sites

Tool	Operating System	Browser
Vischeck	All (web application)	Free
Color Oracle	Mac	Free
colorfilter.wickline.org	All (web application)	Free

Even if a design was tested before being developed, it's a good idea to run it through one of the tools in Table 2-3 anyway. A lot can change between design and deployment, and an innocent request by a customer might have changed a completely accessible design into one that is muddled for certain users. Also, certain items may not have been present in the initial design, such as the effect of mouse-overs or highlighted searches.

Optimization of Images

Unlike image optimization for the blind, not every image on a website needs to be optimized for color blindness. The most important images to optimize are those that convey significant information to the user. Some examples include:

- Scientific images, where important details are indicated by color
- Images with text
- Maps
- Diagrams and graphs
- Images where specific details must not be lost

 Just because the information in the image is spelled out later doesn't mean the image shouldn't be optimized. Forcing a user to read through an entire document to get the information a person without color blindness would get at a glance makes a website much harder for a segment of the population to use.

First, test using a tool that can preview the image in the major kinds of color blindness. This way, you can see if the image actually needs any optimization in the first place. Be careful to note that important areas of the image remain clear and that any color-coding that's been added is still distinct.

If the image does need optimization, it can be run through a tool that changes certain colors to ones that retains high contrast, no matter what type of color blindness (see Table 2-4).

Table 2-4. Tools for optimizing images

Tool	Operating System	Browser
Adobe Photoshop (as of CS5)	Windows / Mac	Approximately $600 (varies by package)
Daltonize	All (web application)	Free

Diagrams, Graphs, and Maps

For stylized graphics, such as maps and icons, a key should be added. Calling something red has little meaning to someone who can't tell red from green. Also, a key still needs to be tested against the various kinds of color blindness. In Figure 2-6, how would someone tell what servers are up and which are down?

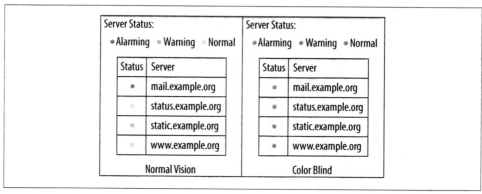

Figure 2-6. Example of bad keys

Another trick for optimizing diagrams, graphs, or maps is to change the line or fill style with each color change. Not only does this help those with color blindness, it helps those who might print out the image, only to discover that they can no longer tell the difference between sections. The map in Figure 2-7 may not have color blindness safe colors, but at least the lines are still distinct.

Tools also exist for creating groups of colors that not only retain high contrast but also retain intensity. If a map is supposed to indicate levels of higher intensity (such as the density of a population) but have inadvertently used a color that is weaker to someone with red-green color blindness, the map becomes deceptive to that user. A popular tool at the moment is Color Brewer 2.0, which includes color schemes that should mesh with nearly every design. Figure 2-8 shows a map from Color Brewer that is extremely color blindness friendly.

The map in Figure 2-8 not only uses colors that are distinctive to all forms of color blindness, but they retain their intensity as well. For maps or graphs that are showing increasing density or percentage, this is vital to keeping the image easy to interpret.

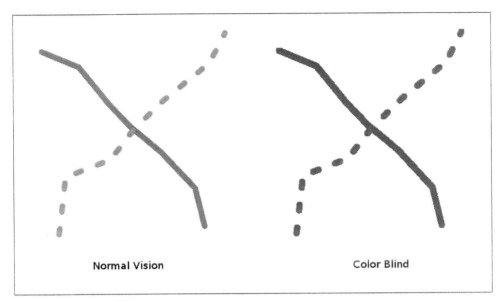

Normal Vision   Color Blind

Figure 2-7. Maps with lines

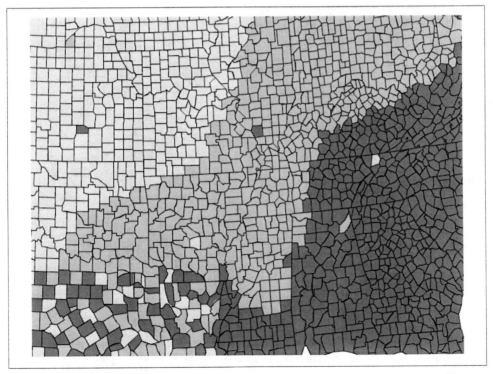

Figure 2-8. Color maps

CHAPTER 3

Audio Accessibility

As browsers have grown more capable, and the average Internet user's bandwidth has gone up, audio has become more vital to using websites. More and more websites include videos, podcasts, and use audio cues to direct users around the site. If a user is unable to hear, they might be left out of vital sections of your website.

Who Does It Cover?

Audio accessibility is more than making websites accessible for the profoundly deaf. This also covers those who are partially deaf and wear hearing aids.

Why can't someone who has only partial hearing loss simply wear headphones? Often, hearing aids and headphones don't mix, even when the headphones go over the ears. Also, some hearing disabled people are deaf only to certain tones, making speech difficult to parse, no matter how loud the volume is.

Additionally, a website owner can't always assume that their users have access to a computer where they can turn the volume up. They might be in a public space where they can't use speakers and don't have headphones, or access to an audio jack.

As with making a site accessible to the blind, the goal to keep in mind for the hearing impaired is to make certain that no vital data is kept from users who cannot hear the audio. This might be more than offering it in text form. If your application has audio indicators, such as a bell, a visual indicator might be required as well.

Annoyances in Brief

People with a hearing disability often have difficulty with the following items:

- Videos with no captioning
- Videos with poor captioning

- Interactive features with no visual alerts
- Poor quality live feeds

Videos

With any video, if there is an audio component, subtitles should be included. Subtitles are more than simply putting the text beneath the image; sounds, cues brought by musical shifts, or tone should be included as well. A good example might be a clip from a horror movie, where tension is built by a change in music, strange noises off screen, or the raspy quality of a voice. Example 3-1 shows how a tense scene might be captioned.

Example 3-1. A script for captioning

```
Woman: Did we lose him?

Man: I think we're alone now. I don't see the killer outside.

(Offscreen: Sound of door opening)

Woman: What was that?!
```

How closed-captioning is implemented is important as well. While it's tempting to simply put text on the bottom of the screen, the text can become obscured if the background matches it too closely. A more elegant solution is to place a band of color at the bottom of the screen and place text on it. This way, the text remains easy to read no matter what happens in the video. Figure 3-1 shows one form of banding, where a minimal amount of the screen is obscured.

Something else to keep in mind when formatting a video for closed-captioning is to make certain that the captions are not covering vital action. A text accompaniment will add nothing if what it's supposed to be describing is hidden from the user. In general, it's better to include the banding beneath the video, so it can't obscure the action. In Figure 3-2, it's impossible for the user to see where the puck is, which is rather important when watching a hockey game.

Figure 3-1. An example of banding

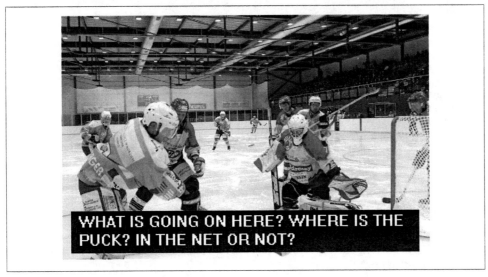

Figure 3-2. An example of obscured action

A number of tools exist for adding closed-captioning to a video, ranging from the enterprise (and costly) to the free and open source. Some services, such as YouTube, also include ways for a user to include their own closed-captioning to uploaded videos.

Most of the tools work in the same way: text can be entered to be displayed at a certain time in the video. After the text is entered, the application might render a new video that includes captioning or provide a file that can be uploaded along with the video.

Even with the captioning taken care of, and the placement such that the action isn't obscured, there is one last visual element to think about: styling. Traditionally, captions were done in all caps in system fonts, with white or colored text on a black background. The combination of these three things makes for something that is incredibly hard to read for extended periods. If you wouldn't design a website this way, why would you do this for captioning?

For captioning, use fonts that are highly readable on a light background. Avoid all caps at all costs, and make certain that all colors used are highly readable. If the text is scrolling by too fast, consider adding more space to the captioning area. Consider the two screens in Figure 3-3. Which one is easier to read?

Figure 3-3. An example of bad styling versus good styling in captioning

After the captions are properly styled, the content of the captioning should be evaluated. Why not just write exactly what the user says? Wouldn't excluding an utterance be keeping a deaf user from content on the site? Not exactly.

When listening, people with normal hearing naturally filter certain snippets of dialog. Those who are reading have no such filtering mechanism. Example 3-2 shows a literal transcript of some public speaking.

Example 3-2. Literal transcript of someone giving a speech

```
MC: Good afternoon, everyone. It's my pleasure to introduce, uh, Cathy Smith.
CS: Oh, ah, thanks everyone. Hmm. Well, today, I've been asked to talk to you about my role
at Cher--- Thermodynamics Inc.
```

Distracting, isn't it? But were someone listening to it, the ers, ahs, and wells would be almost invisible. It's better when transcribing to ignore vocal pauses and verbal missteps, as seen in Example 3-3.

Example 3-3. Transcript of someone giving a speech, cleaned up

```
MC: Good afternoon, everyone. It's my pleasure to introduce Cathy Smith.
CS: Thanks everyone. Today, I've been asked to talk to you about my role at Thermodynamics
Inc.
```

Interactive Features

If your website includes interactive features, such as games or feature explorers, sound often becomes a large part of the experience. In this case, simply captioning might not be enough and might greatly interfere with the feature's design. The goal of someone trying to make these sites compliant should not be to destroy the design but to subtly enhance it.

One place where visual bells are incredibly important are social sites where chat is enabled. Most users are multitasking while on their computer, and naturally drift off to other activities while waiting for someone to respond to them. A user with audio might listen for an alert sound to know that someone has responded to them. How would someone without audio tell that something has happened? In Figures 3-4 through 3-6, a tab in a browser changes color when something has happened that requires the user's attention.

Figure 3-4. Chat, with no alert

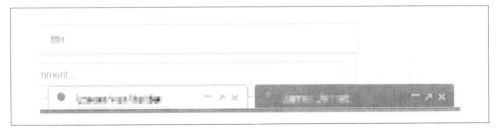

Figure 3-5. Chat, with a visual alert

Figure 3-6. An alert in the browser tab

Unlike videos, if a feature has ambient sounds or background music, these can be safely ignored. Although they do add to the overall experience, they aren't vital to it. Does it matter to a deaf user that your mobile phone explorer has hard rock versus Handel playing? A user probably doesn't need to know that one level of a game has a different loop of background music than another.

If a sound is vital to using the feature, then a visual bell should be added, so that the user knows that something has happened. One method that is difficult to miss is changing the background to a contrasting color for a second, but a solution doesn't need to be so drastic. Many web applications that make sound include a mute button. If a sound is vital to the application, the mute button might flash or display a message.

If an interactive feature has any spoken text, it should follow the rules of videos and always display that text. The style rules, however, can be bent. While the text should always be clear, an interactive feature has more leeway in where the text appears and how it is styled. Adding text doesn't need to make a feature unattractive.

Live Chat

With websites growing more complex, audio chat is becoming a more common feature. Social sites, such as Google Plus or Facebook, now offer ways for people to speak to each other using video and audio rather than through text. Though live transcribing is still a long way in the future, it is possible to make these chats easier on those who cannot hear.

Video chats have become popular with many of those who use sign language. Because of this, if your website features video chats, the quality should be high enough, and the delivery fast enough, so that small motions can be caught. A fuzzy face with blurred hands is useless to someone who is trying to read signs (and is of little use to someone who is looking only at the face for social cues). In Figure 3-7, the speaker's hands are quite blurry, which would make it impossible for two users trying to use sign language to communicate.

The quality and size of a video chat also helps those who read lips. If your site features the option to have multiple people chat at once, be careful about the videos becoming too small. A solution might be to make the video of the speaker appear larger than those that are silent, or allow the user to control who remains large (for instance, the user might care more about what a professor is saying, not what a classmate accidentally said when their mute was off).

Figure 3-7. Blurry hands in a Google Hangout

If your chat features audio, it should also offer a way for users to enter text (see Figure 3-8).

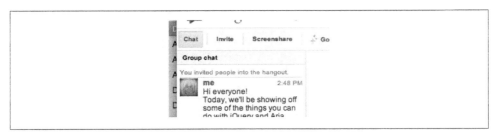

Figure 3-8. Chat box in a Google Hangout

This text chat capability can remain hidden if no one is using it, but if someone does need to use it, there should be some way of indicating that there are text messages to be read. Users who are muted through a disability or equipment problem should not be left completely silenced.

CHAPTER 4

Physical Accessibility

Physical accessibility is slightly different from visual and audio accessibility: the user can see the website and can hear all the audio, so information isn't hidden from them. Making a website physically accessible often boils down to the actual usability of the website. How hard is it to navigate? Are applications frustrating to use? This, of all the types of accessibility, benefits the most, as the guidelines laid out make a better experience for even typical users.

Who Does It Cover?

Physical accessibility covers any user who might have trouble using traditional forms of input for their computer. This can range from those who are paralyzed to those who have broken their dominant arm and must use their off hand to use a mouse. Following a few standards also helps those who are suffering from a broken trackpad or mouse, and have to use a keyboard as their only navigation. Some common use cases:

- A disorder might cause shaking or jerking, such as some forms of cerebral palsy and Parkinsons.
- A disorder might slow the user's motions, such as some forms of cerebral palsy and some brain traumas.
- A user might have lost the use of a dominant limb, causing them to lose accuracy while learning to use their non-dominant limb.
- A user might be completely unable to use a mouse, but still have use of their keyboard. Sites would be navigated by tabbing through the elements, or using arrow keys.

Those that are physically disabled might use a variety of alternate devices:

- Eye-tracking devices, that move a mouse based on where the user is looking
- Keyboard-only inputs, when a user cannot use a mouse

- One-handed keyboards, which may make certain combinations of keys impossible
- Mice that are set up for those who might shake or jerk

It's important to keep in mind that in spite of the availability of specialized equipment, a physically disabled user might be forced to use a less-than-optimal setup. Like screen readers for the blind, a developer cannot assume that a user has the latest and greatest equipment.

Annoyances in Brief

Those with physical disabilities often have trouble with the following:

- Interfaces that require the mouse
- Interfaces that require the keyboard
- Items that need a high level of precision
- Items that trigger easily, but are difficult to close

Best Practices

Forms

If your site includes a form, there's a good chance it includes radio buttons or check boxes. Checking on the box or button itself is difficult for someone with a motion disorder (and can be annoying for a user with normal motion control). There are typically two solutions to this issue: be tab- and arrow-friendly, and allow the user to click on the text of an item to make a selection.

Making a form tab-friendly comes down to making certain all form fields are accessible through pressing the Tab key, and that the fields are tabbed to in a sensible order.

Also, forms should be one element after another on a page rather than elements placed next to each other, like they might be on a paper form. If a user is tabbing, they shouldn't have to hunt for where their cursor went. Figures 4-1 and 4-2 show forms with poor layout and good layout.

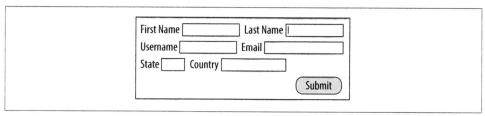

Figure 4-1. A bad form has fields on the same line

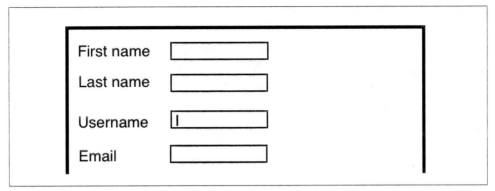

Figure 4-2. A good form has one field per line

A form with fields displayed vertically is much easier for most people to follow and has a more predictable tab order.

If, for whatever reason, your form must have elements next to each other, then the tab order should take the user through the form from left to right, as they might read it. This is done by adding a `tabindex` attribute to the inputs, as seen in Example 4-1.

Example 4-1. TABINDEX

```
<form action="..." method="post">
    <p>
        <input tabindex="1" type="text" name="field1" />
        <input tabindex="2" type="text" name="field2" />
        <input tabindex="3" type="submit" name="submit" />
    </p>
</form>
```

With radio buttons, tabbing to that form element should hit only the first of the radio elements. If the user hits Tab again, she should move to the next form element, not the next radio button. The user would select a radio element by using arrow keys rather than by using tab. This allows her to move around the form quickly, rather than getting caught up in a long radio list. Example 4-2 shows how `tabindex` can be added to radio buttons within a form.

Example 4-2. TABINDEX and radio buttons

```
<form>
    <input tabindex="1" type="text name="Full name" />
    <input tabindex="2" type="radio" name="sex" value="Male" /> Male <br />
    <input type="radio" name="sex" value="Female" /> Female <br />
</form>
```

The same is also true for groups of check boxes, as seen in Example 4-3. The user should not be forced to tab through each one. Add a `tabindex` only to the first one, ignoring the rest.

Example 4-3. TABINDEX and check boxes

```
<form>
    <input tabindex="1" type="text" name="Favorite Game" />
    <input tabindex="2" type="checkbox" name="system" value="xbox360">XBox 360 />
    <input type="checkbox" name="system" value="PS3" />PS3
    <input type="checkbox" name="system" value="Wii" />Wii
</form>
```

Even with the ability to skip sections of a form, a section with too many elements can become tedious for a user without a mouse. While there is no hard and fast rule, if a set of radio buttons has become tiresome to arrow through, it's best to replace it with a select drop-down. These can be navigated quickly by typing into them, if they're set up correctly.

Since a user can start typing and get to the element she wants, it's best if the items don't begin with redundant information. As seen in Figure 4-3, if you have a list of teams from several sports, don't start with the sport name. Begin with the team name, which is unique. This way, the user isn't forced to type the sport name and any separators before getting to her selection.

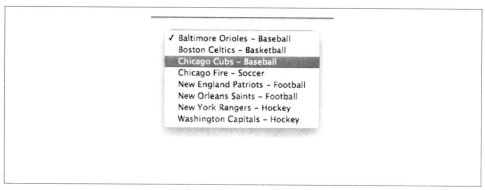

Figure 4-3. Drop-down uniqueness

One unfortunate side effect to doing this is that elements are no longer as visually ordered as they might have been before. One solution to use group entries using OPTGROUP, shown in Example 4-4. The items will appear together under the OPTGROUP heading, but the heading itself won't be selectable. A user can still type to move quickly around the form.

Example 4-4. Using OPTGROUP

```
<select name="color" id="color">

<optgroup label="Blue-Greens">
```

```
        <option value="bgteal">Teal</option>
        <option value="bgcyan">Cyan</option>
        <option value="bgaqua">Aqua</option>

</optgroup>

<optgroup label="Reds">

        <option value="rscarlet">Scarlet</option>
        <option value="rvermillion">Vermillion</option>
        <option value="rcrimson">Crimson</option>

</optgroup>

</select>
```

Appears as:

Pop-Ups

Pop-ups, whether a purposeful part of a web application or as a form of advertising, can pose a special challenge to users with motion disorders. Not only can they switch the user's focus, but they can be difficult to close. Figure 4-4 shows a pop-up that is not only easy to trigger (it comes up when the user mouses over a link), but it's also difficult to close, since it requires clicking on a rather small button.

Pop-ups that open in their own windows pose the least issues. While potentially annoying, these can be closed with a simple keyboard command. With advancing browser capabilities, however, many web applications now have pop-ups appear within the current window, ensuring that they get the user's attention. Many times, they will require the user to click a small X to close them, something that can be incredibly difficult for a user with a motion disorder. If these pop-ups occur due to a roll-over, this can be even more frustrating, as a shaky user might have trouble avoiding these rollovers.

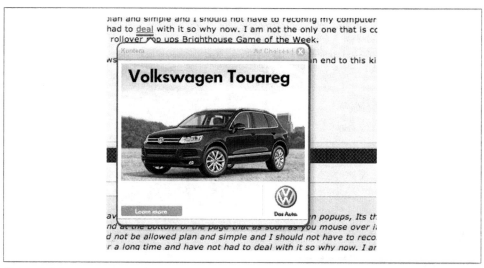

Figure 4-4. In-page pop-up advertising

Purposeful pop-ups can also be problematic. If the user is using a keyboard to navigate, it's possible that he won't be able to tab to the pop-up, rendering the site unusable. If the pop-up must be closed by hitting a button, and the button is small, a user using a mouse would the same issues as he would above.

Do these annoyances mean pop-ups should never be used? No, but they should be crafted carefully so as not to annoy users. A well-designed pop-up can be a boon to a website, for any user.

The first thing to consider is how the user is to close the window. Keep in mind that the user can be using either a mouse or a keyboard to navigate the site. For the keyboard users, the most elegant solution (that is also helpful to typical users) is to allow the user to close the window with a keystroke. The ESC key is a popular choice, as it doesn't require dexterous hands to hit two keys at once. Whatever key is chosen, however, do not depend on the popularity of your choice: make certain to spell out that the user can hit it to close the window. Example 4-5 shows some sample code for closing a window upon hitting ESC.

Example 4-5. Code sample: hitting ESC to close a pop-up

```
$(document).keydown(function(e) {
    // ESCAPE key pressed
    if (e.keyCode == 27) {
        window.close();
    }
});
```

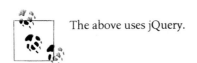 The above uses jQuery.

If the user is using a mouse, keep in mind that he may not have the option of using a keyboard, or using a keyboard may be extremely difficult for him. This is why a visual indicator should always be included with any pop-up. Ideally, the indicator should be large enough for a user to click, even with an unpredictable pointer, but not so large as to disrupt the design.

In general, an icon that is 13x13 pixels should be large enough for those with motion issues. As an additional advantage, it's large enough for those using touch screens, which includes adaptive devices as well as tablets.

Navigation

Elements that drop down have become increasingly popular in the world of web design. This allows for a clean high-level navigation that can easily get the user to deeper sections of the site, or allow them to browse the site's content without having to load a new page. These navigations, however, can be problematic for a user who is struggling to use a mouse. With CSS and modern browsers, they've become incredibly simple to make, helping their propagation on the Internet.

One common feature that quickly becomes an issue is a menu that snaps back like a rubber band if the mouse moves off of the menu. A user with an unsteady hand might have finally navigated to the element he wants, only to have it disappear due to an involuntary tremor. He must then return to the original navigation element to try again.

A more user-friendly behavior would be menus that stay dropped down once they have been activated, or that at least have tolerance for a wavering mouse.

Superfish (*http://users.tpg.com.au/j_birch/plugins/superfish/*) is one library that offers extremely tolerant drop-downs. When a user triggers a drop-down, the menu comes down. If the user's mouse wavers off of it, it stays down for several seconds before fading away.

If a sticky or tolerant drop-down can't be incorporated, at the very least consider having only one level of drop-downs. This way, the user won't be frustrated by carefully navigating several sets of sub-menus, only to lose his progress. These are a boon to users with normal mouse control, as drop-down menus that are overly complex can be aggravating to any user.

If a user isn't using a mouse, but is instead tabbing through the site, all elements, including the drop-down elements, need to be available. If a user tabs onto an element that has drop-down items, those items should show immediately, as seen in Figure 4-5. Should he hit Tab again, those items should be cycled through (hitting the down arrow key would just move the entire page down). This is another reason not to make drop-down navigation too complex: it would take a keyboard dependent user too long to move through it.

Figure 4-5. Tabbing through navigation

Moving around the Page

One distressing phenomenon that's been spreading through the design community is the tendency to set outline to none in a site's global CSS. The code shown in Example 4-6 should never be introduced into a site's code base.

Example 4-6. What not to do with the outline attribute

```
:focus {
    outline: 0;
    }
```

Designers usually reason that outline can be overridden in other parts of the CSS. Most CSS resets will include setting outline to zero, with a reminder to the designer to add focus back in. Most never do.

What does focus do? It allows a keyboard user to move around a page to see where her current focus is. Links or items that have focus will have a faint outline around them, as seen in Figure 4-6.

This outline can be styled by the designer, but if it's set to 0, nothing will be displayed. The outline should, at the very least, be left alone. If it must be styled, then it should be obvious where the user's focus is. It should never be completely obliterated.

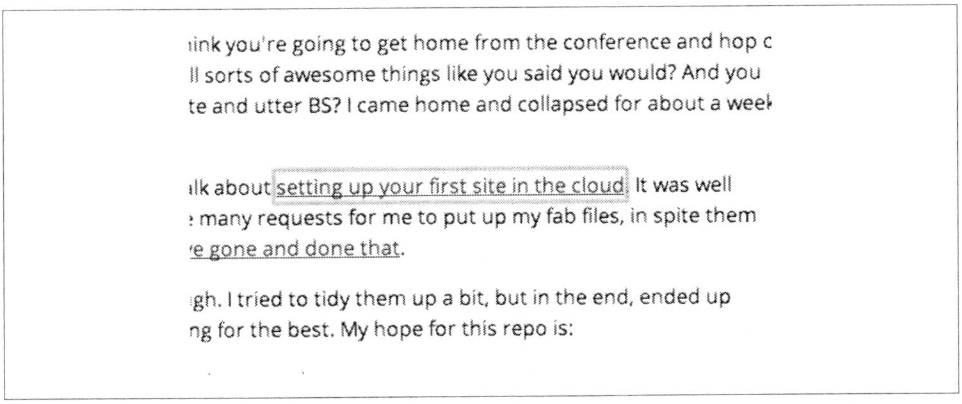

ink you're going to get home from the conference and hop c
ll sorts of awesome things like you said you would? And you
te and utter BS? I came home and collapsed for about a week

ilk about setting up your first site in the cloud. It was well
; many requests for me to put up my fab files, in spite them
'e gone and done that.

gh. I tried to tidy them up a bit, but in the end, ended up
ng for the best. My hope for this repo is:

Figure 4-6. An unstyled focus

Timing

It's important to keep in mind that a user with a physical disability might be slower at inputting data than a typical user. While this doesn't affect most websites, there are some use cases where timing is important. For example, a site that sells tickets to a popular event might allow a user only a set amount of time to enter their information and submit payment. Another might use a CAPTCHA to ensure that the user isn't a robot, but the CAPTCHA must be filled in before too long or the user will be timed out.

If a feature of your application requires that the user be timed, try to be generous with that amount of time. If a typical user can fill out the form in 5 minutes, try allowing much more than that, like 15. If this would break the application, then allow the user to request more time and be clear that the form is being timed and what the consequences are if time runs out.

If the form times out, try to retain all the content of the form so that the user can at least try again. While sensitive data, such as credit card information, may need to be removed, see if it's possible to simply obscure it. Move the user to the top of the form, showing a summary of reasons why her form wasn't submitted, and clearly show which fields must be filled out again.

Also, consider removing timeouts altogether, if the application can tolerate it. Does a comment form need a CAPTCHA that times out after just a few minutes? Can an alternative method of catching spam be used?

Testing

Testing a site for accessibility for physical disabilities comes down to using the site with the similar restrictions as someone who has issues using a mouse or is completely dependent on the keyboard. Unlike testing for the blind, however, there are few, if any, currently available applications that test for physical accessibility. This is left completely up to the tester.

Testing Without a Mouse

Emulating a user who cannot use a mouse is very easy: the tester should disable his mouse. Though simply not using it is an option, many people are so used to using a mouse that they reach for it instinctively. Unplugging it and disabling any trackpads ensures that the tester cannot accidentally use a mouse to get out of a sticky situation.

After the mouse has been disabled, the tester should attempt to navigate the site using only tabs and arrow keys. Some things to take note of:

- Can the tester get to all items in the navigation?
- If there is a form, can the user get to all items in the form?
- Is the form order logical, or does the focus move around the page?
- If the form is timed, how much time is allotted for the user? Can the user tell how much time they have to submit a form?
- After letting a form fail, is it easy for the user to resubmit the form?

Testing for Uneven Pointers

Some users will still choose to use a mouse, but due to a motion disorder, won't have the accuracy of a typical user. One of the simplest ways to emulate these issues is for the tester to use his or her mouse...but with their non-dominant hand (if the tester is ambidextrous, this obviously won't work). To emulate a user with a steady but slower hand, increase the sensitivity of the mouse to the maximum the system allows.

These methods are imperfect, but they do allow the tester to truly evaluate how difficult using a website might be for this kind of user. Some things to consider:

- If there are drop-down menus on the site, how long do they stay down after the mouse has moved on? How many levels are there to the drop-down menus?
- If there are pop-ups, how difficult is it to close them? How long does it take, compared to a typical user?
- On forms, does clicking the text for a check box select or deselect the check box?
- On forms, does clicking the text for a radio button select that radio button?

Cognitive Disabilities

Overview

Recently, another group has become more vocal in their need for an accessible web: those with cognitive disorders. These can include:

- Those with mild to severe dyslexia
- Those with attention-deficit disorders, such as ADD or ADHD
- Anyone with an information-processing disorder

Dyslexia

Dyslexia is often characterized as people who simply transpose numbers or letters now and then. This couldn't be further from the truth: dyslexia, like most conditions, ranges from a mild disability to an extremely disabling one, with some people being more strongly affected in some areas than others. It can range from those who can cope in everyday life to those who are rendered functionally illiterate. Some describe letters that move around and swap as they look at them. Others describe words becoming blocks of color.

The effects of dyslexia can go beyond reading. Many find it disrupts their ability to organize information, or keep a virtual map in their head. They complain of headaches and not being able to focus. How can we make a website, which is made of words, easier for someone who has issues with words themselves?

Fonts

People with dyslexia often report that the universally reviled font Comic Sans is easier to read. They reported that the letters seemed to stay in place better, with rotations and flipping happening less often. Why?

It's common when designing fonts to simply take one character and flip it about to make four letters. b, p, d, and q are commonly created by rotating and flipping a single letter, leaving less work for the designer, and making a font that appears more even. This can cause issues for those with dyslexia, as this makes the letters even more easy to swap while trying to read them.

As a result, many people with dyslexia prefer fonts where all the letters are unique. Comic Sans, with its hand-drawn letters, fits the bill. Does this mean you should replace Helvetica with Comic Sans? Of course not. Besides, better fonts than Comic Sans have been created in the past few years for dyslexics, but they're not available on all computers, nor are they available for embedding.

Many dyslexics will often use a custom style sheet to restyle fonts on websites to be more readable for them. Allowing these style sheets goes a long way to making your website more usable for this group. If text is embedded in an image, obviously, it can't be restyled.

Unfortunately, navigation is a popular place for websites to have images with text. With more and more browsers accepting web fonts, text is becoming easier to style outside of Photoshop. Figure 5-1 shows a navigation created using webfonts. Google offers a number of web fonts, free to use, as do sites such as Font Squirrel. Even better, the font is often smaller than a handful of image files for inactive, active, and roll-over states.

Figure 5-1. An example of navigation using a webfont

In the header:

```
<link href='http://fonts.googleapis.com/css?family=Fascinate+Inline'
rel='stylesheet' type='text/css'>
```

In the CSS:

```
ul.nav { ... font-family: 'Fascinate Inline', cursive; ... }
```

In the HTML for the navigation:

```
<ul class="nav">
        <li class="active"><a href="#">Home</a></li>
        <li><a href="#about">About</a></li>
        <li><a href="#contact">Contact</a></li>
</ul>
```

Here are some sources for web fonts (Table 5-1):

Table 5-1. Sources for Web Fonts

Site Name	URL	License
Google Web Fonts	*http://www.google.com/webfonts/*	Free
Font Squirrel	*http://www.fontsquirrel.com/*	Free
Font Spring	*http://www.fontspring.com/*	Pay per font, unlimited
Typekit	*http://typekit.com/*	Subscription-based, limited page views
Fonts.com	*http://www.fonts.com/web-fonts/*	Free, Subscription-, and fee-based, limited page views

Just because a user is usually able to use a custom stylesheet, however, is no reason to think that they will always be able to do so. A dyslexic user might have to use a computer in a library or in a work environment that has locked down this feature. They might be working on a new system and don't have access to their custom stylesheet. A web application might force them to use a browser that doesn't support custom style sheets. Consider someone with only mild dyslexia who chooses not to use custom style sheets. How can a website's fonts be chosen so that they still support these users?

Sans serif fonts have shown themselves to be easier for those with dyslexia to read than serif fonts. Helvetica, already popular on many websites, is a good choice, as is Verdana or Arial. Fonts with serifs, or that have uneven spacing between letters, can be more difficult to read. Examples of serif and sans serif fonts are shown in Figure 5-2.

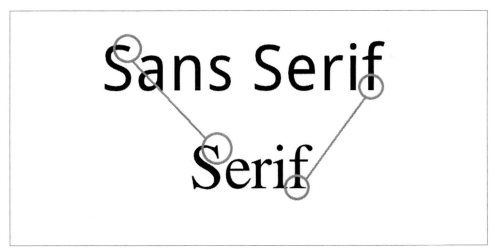

Figure 5-2. Serif and Sans Serif Fonts

It's important to note that sans serif fonts have proven the easiest for most people to read on a screen. Using them for all of a website's large blocks of text improves the experience for everyone.

Content

Sentence length

Sentences should be kept short. Although there's no hard and fast rule, 10–15 words per sentence is likely be comfortable enough for dyslexics and the common population alike.

Paragraph length

In early grade school, many students are taught that a paragraph should be five sentences long: an opening statement, at least three facts, and a closing statement. While practical for that venue, this rule is best thrown out when it comes to writing content for the web that's easy to consume.

When dealing with people who are reading on a screen, shorter paragraphs are easier to focus on. Although an idea might be spread out over several paragraphs, retention will actually increase due to the information being put into smaller pieces (a process that's sometimes referred to as "chunking").

Color Choice

While high contrast is often considered the best choice, those with dyslexia actually have issues with colors that are too high contrast. Pure black on pure white can cause text to blur, rendering a site nearly impossible to read. A better choice is off-black against off-white (for example, #111 on #eee). Not only is this easier for dyslexics to read, it's also shown to lead to less eye strain in the rest of the population.

Justified Text

Justified text, which fills content areas from side to side perfectly, is a common choice made by designers. They lead to attractive webpages with content evenly blocked out. Justified text also wreaks havoc on people with dyslexia.

How does it affect a user with dyslexia? Justified text creates more whitespace in order to have text fit exactly between two margins. This whitespace is often perceived as a single unit, an effect called "The River Effect" by typographers, displayed in Figure 5-3. Dyslexic readers report being distracted by these gaps: some reporting seeing them move, with others reporting that the gaps distract them as they try to make out the shape of words.

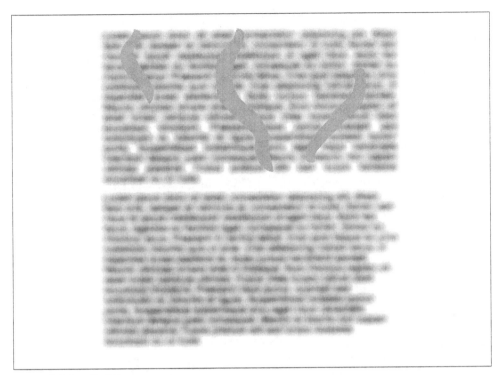

Figure 5-3. Justified Text

The simplest solution is to leave out fully justified text completely from all stylesheets. In spite of its more professional look, it adds nothing to the readability of a website. Even users without dyslexia can find it annoying. Unlike a printed document, different browsers and screen resolutions will execute the justification differently. Some might add more whitespace than others, others might add whitespace only between words, and others may add whitespace between the letters themselves.

Images

Images can be both a boon and burden to dyslexic users. Many people with dyslexia report that they think with images, so having meaningful graphics on a website can help a dyslexic user retain more of the site's content. On the other hand, images can also distract a dyslexic user to the point of making a site unusable.

Meaningful Images

Images that are meaningful to the content of a webpage can serve two purposes: one, to break up long sections of content; and two, to give the user a marker that allows them to quickly find content that is meaningful to them.

Long blocks of text, even when separated out into paragraphs, can be tiring for someone with dyslexia. A well-chosen graphic can help distill the meaning of the text around it, giving the user an anchor as they take in information.

Meaningful images can also help a user who is trying to scan a page for meaningful content. Unlike users without dyslexia, a dyslexic user has trouble scanning blocks of text for meaningful keywords. For example, if a dyslexic user is scanning a webpage of available services at a university, and looking for dining services, an icon of a plate and fork, or the image of a student eating, will stand out much faster than the text label 'Dining Services.'

Adding images to navigation can help dyslexic user as well. This allows them to skip reading text, seeking out the icons instead as they move around the website. Figure 5-4 shows several how icons have been used to enhance a site's navigation.

Figure 5-4. Navigation with icons

Animations

Animations—whether animated GIFs, JavaScript, or Flash—can be a terrible distraction for a user with dyslexia. If a website has enough of them, it can be rendered completely unusable.

In general, animations distract any user from the content of a web page. People with dyslexia have additional issues with visual attention. Whereas a normal user might, with effort, eventually block out an annoying animation, a dyslexic user might be distracted by it every time it loops. Many times, issues with attention aren't about not noticing something, but about noticing too much and being unable to block it out.

Animations with meaning

Animations aren't always a poor choice. A well-designed animation can add more meaning and value to a page than thousands of lines of text. With some care, these animations can be added to a page without causing undue stress to a dyslexic reader.

If possible, show the animation statically until the user chooses to animate it. Movies shouldn't autoplay and interactive features should remain as static as possible until the user chooses to interact with them. If possible, animated GIFs should animate only on mouseover. Example 5-1 contains some sample JavaScript for animating on mouse over.

Example 5-1. Animating on mouse over

```
<html>

  <head>
    <script type="text/javascript" src="jquery.js"></script>
    <script type="text/javascript">
      $(function() {
        $("#hurricane").hover(

          function() {
            $(this).attr("src", "Animated_hurricane.gif");
          },

          function() {
            $(this).attr("src", "still_hurricane.gif");
          }
          );
      });
    </script>
    <head>
      <body>
        <img id="hurricane" src="still_hurricane.gif">
      </body>
</html>
```

If the mouseover option isn't a possibility for an animated GIF, consider having the image load only when a link is clicked. The image can load in another window, which the user can close when he's done with it.

Advertisements

Today, most websites pull in a significant amount of revenue from advertisements from a third-party vendor. This puts most website owners in a precarious situation: someone else is choosing what content gets loaded on their website with every user. This content is designed to attract attention. Can a website with advertisements still be made accessible to those with dyslexia?

One option is to carefully vet third-party advertisers, if possible.

- Can the site owner request that advertisements never play sound (unless the user explicitly asks them to)?
- Is there an option to display only static ads?
- Can the site owner request ads with animations to loop only once?
- Can particularly annoying vendors be blocked?

Some site owners might have little or no say over which vendors they use. Can these websites be made accessible for dyslexia? What if they're stuck with someone who will serve only endlessly looping, distracting ads?

If the site owner has control over where the ads are placed, one option is to make certain that the user can either move past them or hide them by changing the size of the screen.

If an ad is to be displayed horizontally within the content of a page, make certain the user can position the page so that the image isn't on the screen (Figure 5-5). Even if the ad is distracting, a dyslexic user will have the option to scroll the page up or down to hide it. Make certain not to have page content to the left or right of the ad, so the user doesn't lose any content if she hides the ad.

Figure 5-5. Ad space that can be hidden by scrolling

If an ad is a vertical—or column—ad, the user can't scroll past it without losing significant chunks of content. In this instance, it's better to align these ads to the right side of the page, as seen in Figure 5-6. The user can than make his browser screen narrower, moving the ads off screen. Check to make certain that the page's styling isn't too flexible, though. The main content (sometimes called the content well) of a page should have a minimum width, so that resizing the browser window won't cause the web page to be rendered more and more narrowly.

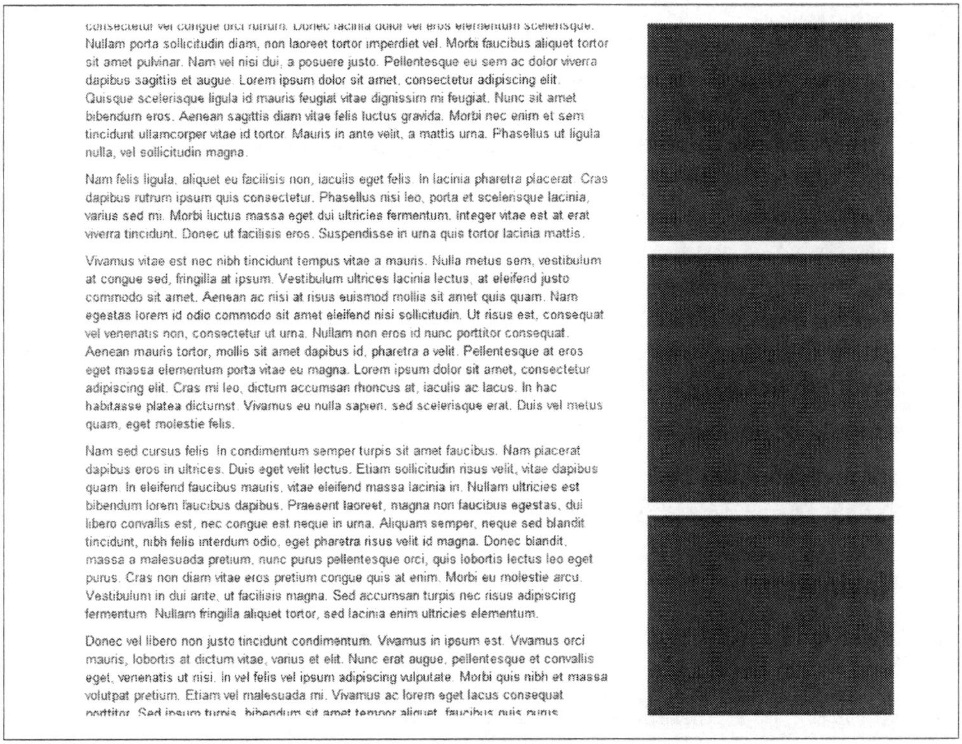

consectetur vel congue orci rutrum. Donec lacinia dolor vel eros elementum scelerisque. Nullam porta sollicitudin diam, non laoreet tortor imperdiet vel. Morbi faucibus aliquet tortor sit amet pulvinar. Nam vel nisi dui, a posuere justo. Pellentesque eu sem ac dolor viverra dapibus sagittis et augue. Lorem ipsum dolor sit amet, consectetur adipiscing elit. Quisque scelerisque ligula id mauris feugiat vitae dignissim mi feugiat. Nunc sit amet bibendum eros. Aenean sagittis diam vitae felis luctus gravida. Morbi nec enim et sem tincidunt ullamcorper vitae id tortor. Mauris in ante velit, a mattis urna. Phasellus ut ligula nulla, vel sollicitudin magna.

Nam felis ligula, aliquet eu facilisis non, iaculis eget felis. In lacinia pharetra placerat. Cras dapibus rutrum ipsum quis consectetur. Phasellus nisi leo, porta et scelensque lacinia, varius sed mi. Morbi luctus massa eget dui ultricies fermentum. Integer vitae est at erat viverra tincidunt. Donec ut facilisis eros. Suspendisse in urna quis tortor lacinia mattis.

Vivamus vitae est nec nibh tincidunt tempus vitae a mauris. Nulla metus sem, vestibulum at congue sed, fringilla at ipsum. Vestibulum ultrices lacinia lectus, at eleifend justo commodo sit amet. Aenean ac nisi at risus euismod mollis sit amet quis quam. Nam egestas lorem id odio commodo sit amet eleifend nisi sollicitudin. Ut risus est, consequat vel venenatis non, consectetur ut urna. Nullam non eros id nunc porttitor consequat. Aenean mauris tortor, mollis sit amet dapibus id, pharetra a velit. Pellentesque at eros eget massa elementum porta vitae eu magna. Lorem ipsum dolor sit amet, consectetur adipiscing elit. Cras mi leo, dictum accumsan rhoncus at, iaculis ac lacus. In hac habitasse platea dictumst. Vivamus eu nulla sapien, sed scelerisque erat. Duis vel metus quam, eget molestie felis.

Nam sed cursus felis. In condimentum semper turpis sit amet faucibus. Nam placerat dapibus eros in ultrices. Duis eget velit lectus. Etiam sollicitudin risus velit, vitae dapibus quam. In eleifend faucibus mauris, vitae eleifend massa lacinia in. Nullam ultricies est bibendum lorem faucibus dapibus. Praesent laoreet, magna non faucibus egestas, dui libero convallis est, nec congue est neque in urna. Aliquam semper, neque sed blandit tincidunt, nibh felis interdum odio, eget pharetra risus velit id magna. Donec blandit, massa a malesuada pretium, nunc purus pellentesque orci, quis lobortis lectus leo eget purus. Cras non diam vitae eros pretium congue quis at enim. Morbi eu molestie arcu. Vestibulum in dui ante, ut facilisis magna. Sed accumsan turpis nec risus adipiscing fermentum. Nullam fringilla aliquet tortor, sed lacinia enim ultricies elementum.

Donec vel libero non justo tincidunt condimentum. Vivamus in ipsum est. Vivamus orci mauris, lobortis at dictum vitae, varius et elit. Nunc erat augue, pellentesque et convallis eget, venenatis ut nisi. In vel felis vel ipsum adipiscing vulputate. Morbi quis nibh et massa volutpat pretium. Etiam vel malesuada mi. Vivamus ac lorem eget lacus consequat porttitor. Sed ipsum turpis, bibendum sit amet tempor aliquet, faucibus quis purus.

Figure 5-6. Ad space that can be hidden by resizing the browser

What if a website uses responsive design, where resizing the browser changes the layout of the page? If the ads are still included in the narrower version of the page, make certain that they're displayed with no text surrounding them, still allowing the user to scroll past them.

Backgrounds

Though graphical backgrounds can increase branding and interest for a web page, they can be distracting for someone with dyslexia and might also render text unreadable. The best practice is to never have images behind text. No matter how subtle the pattern is, it can make it more difficult to make out the word shape.

Alt text

Some users' dyslexia is so severe that they prefer to use a specialized screen reader that will read websites aloud to them. They share many of the features of screen readers for the blind, while also tracking visually where a user is in a block of text.

These screen readers will also read alt text for images, so if an image must have text in it, make certain that the text is represented in the image's alt text.

Print Versions

Some people with dyslexia report problems dealing with computer screens, citing visual stress. Some cope by using transparent overlays that are tinted to make text easier to read. Others choose to print out websites with large blocks of text, so having a print version is vital to these users.

A sans serif font should be used (if it isn't already). Though some designers prefer a serif font for print, the studies on readability of serif versus sans serif for typical users are less clear cut than many would believe. There's little evidence that one is better than the other for users without an information processing disorder. Since one isn't clearly better than the other, why not favor the font family that is demonstrably better for people with dyslexia?

Fonts should be no smaller than 12pt, with 14pt being preferable.

Lines of text shouldn't be any longer than 60 to 70 characters. It's tempting to make use of the full page to save on paper, but doing so wouldn't benefit a dyslexic user.

Site Navigation

Moving around a website can be troublesome for someone with dyslexia, especially if a website owner has decided to take a non-traditional approach to their navigation.

Navigation can be an underappreciated aspect of a website. Some designers have even advocated removing it altogether, noting that most visitors seem to come in search results and barely click around at all. Why keep it around? Why not link to other relevant pieces of content and have a site search?

Navigation helps every visitor understand the context of a website. Even if a user never clicks anything in the navigation, it's almost guaranteed that they look at it. Navigation helps the user understand who is hosting this content (Is it a blog, or a major corporation?). It can help the user guess who the audience is, and if the site might meet their needs (Is it written for the technical community, or for more casual users?) It also helps them keep track of where they are within the overall structure of the website.

Given that, what elements of navigation are most important to someone with dyslexia?

One of the most important features is global navigation. The navigation should not change as the user moves through the site; it should always display the top-level categories for the website and be as simple as possible. Showing the user their current category through styling can also be helpful, but the content should always remain the same. Mozilla has a particularly elegant solution: a simple navigation that expands to display more of the site structure (Figure 5-7).

Figure 5-7. Mozilla's Global Navigation

A site map is often used as a back-up, if a dyslexic user can't find what she wants through the main navigation. This way, she can read through a list of subcategories and articles in a website, in hopes of finding something relevant to what she wants. If a website includes a site map, it should be a part of one of the global navigations.

Search, while popular for many users, is especially problematic for those with dyslexia. Search can be of limited help to someone who has issues with transposing letters or guessing the spelling of an unfamiliar word. Adding spell check to a site's search engine can help, but many people with dyslexia will choose not to use it at all.

Site-specific back and forward navigation is something that's common on many complex web applications. These are especially annoying to dyslexic users, who are already using a sizable amount of mental energy processing text and remembering where they are within the site. Now, they have to remember not to use their browser's back and forward buttons. Chances are, they'll forget, and lose their place.

If possible, never insist that a user use a web application's back and forward buttons. The frustration it brings to any user isn't worth it.

ADD and ADHD

ADHD (Attention Deficit Hyperactivity Disorder) and ADD (Attention Deficit Disorder) are most commonly characterized as disorders that affect only children. Many of these children, however, never grow out of ADD/ADHD, carrying it into adulthood. It is estimated that 4% of adults in the United States have some form of ADD or ADHD (known collectively as AD/HD).

ADD and ADHD are cognitive disorders that lead to issues with attention, and in the case of ADHD, hyperactivity. Although it may seem as though someone with AD/HD has trouble paying attention, the truth is that they have trouble paying attention to too much. Adults with AD/HD often describe being in a world where everything seems to happen at once, or where they don't feel fully in control of what their brain is doing. They also describe moments of incredible focus, where the world around them seems to fade away, to the point where loved ones or alarms can't break through the fugue. Waiting is difficult. Completing mundane tasks is impossible.

While AD/HD is often treated with stimulants, some adults might not be able to take the medications due to other conditions, expense of the medication, or preference for other therapies. Also, if a user is diagnosed as an adult, the issues gained in childhood cannot be fully compensated for by medication. They still have issues with organization and retention, even if they've gained the ability to pay attention for longer spans of time.

Similarity to Dyslexia

While AD/HD and dyslexia are two disorders that have vastly different symptoms, there is some overlap in designing for the two groups. Because both groups have issues with attention, if a website is accessible to one group, it's often accessible to the other group.

The following items benefit both groups:

- Sentence and paragraph length: Both should be kept short.
- Animations: Animations should be kept to a minimum, and shouldn't autoplay, if possible.
- Backgrounds: Should be kept simple and muted, with content appearing with no background at all.
- Navigation: Should be global and consistent.

Timed Tasks

People with AD/HD often report needing to take breaks or requiring more time to complete tasks due to getting distracted. Although most websites are fine with users taking their time, sometimes a task becomes time sensitive. A long form might time out if a user spends too much time filling it out or wanders away from the task. Even a short form with a timer (for example, one used to purchase tickets for a concert) can be problematic if a user with AD/HD gets distracted in the middle of filling it out.

For longer forms, consider giving users the ability to save their progress, or auto-saving for them as they move through the form. That way, if the user finds that they must take a break, they can return to the form later without losing their place.

Also, if possible, break a long form into smaller sections, with a clear indication of how far they have to go in order to complete the form. Smaller chunks are easier to focus on and present fewer distractions to the user. A progress bar, as seen in Figure 5-8, can be a simple yet effective way to communicate to the user how much further they have to go. The user can then better pace themselves through a task they might find uninteresting.

Figure 5-8. Progress bar for a multi-page form

Before declaring a short form fine for people with attention disorders, try filling it out and leaving it. How long can you let it sit before the submit button no longer works?

Instructions

Following instructions can be problematic for those with AD/HD. It can be difficult for them to focus long enough to fully comprehend them, and if the instructions are complex, they might have issues keeping track of their progress.

If necessary, a website's instructions should be kept as clear and short as possible. Any words not necessary to the meaning of the instructions should be removed, and if possible, the instructions should be formatted as a list rather than in a block.

It's becoming increasingly popular for websites to use videos instead of text to present instructions. This can be both a boon and a burden to users with AD/HD. Some respond better to audio and visual cues, so the videos might be a better resource for them. Others get distracted by the visual elements of videos, or might have issues with auditory processing. If a website has instructional videos, the instructions also need to be presented in a written format that is more than just a transcript of the video. If a user didn't have the video at all, he should still be able to use the instructions to get what he needs. Incidentally, this also benefits someone using a mobile device that can't display that type of video.

Organization

Any user will benefit from a well-organized website, but users with AD/HD are especially sensitive to material that's poorly organized or pages that include too much information.

An overly long page can be problematic for a user with AD/HD. They may lose track of where they were and be forced to start over from the beginning. If possible, try to break up long pages into a multi-page format, where each unit makes sense as a whole. Adding random breaks is less helpful than breaking up an article into subsections. For example, a page about Chicago might be broken into pages about its history, local geography, politics, and tourism.

It's important to note that the multi-page format is somewhat controversial for some users. Try to include the option to see all the sections on one page, or make breaking up the page into sections an option, with the single-page format being default.

If information is particularly important, it shouldn't be buried in a mound of text. It should be highlighted in some manner, perhaps by using a callout to call attention to it or by putting the text in bold. At the very least, it should be presented in its own paragraph or at the beginning of a new paragraph.

Consistent User Experience

No user likes to be needlessly surprised by an interface, but this can be especially trying for those with AD/HD. For a user with a mind that's already predisposed to distraction, an interface that suddenly changes can make a site incredibly difficult to use.

Many times, one website is actually a group of independent web applications, loosely sewn together under one domain. Each of the application owners need to make certain that some things remain consistent:

- Does the overall look and feel of the site remain the same? Is it really that important that each section of a website have a drastically different style?
- Does the global navigation remain the same, with the only change being to show where someone is within the overall architecture of the site?
- Is information presented in a consistent way, or do tools in one section disappear in another? Are some stories broken up, while others are all on one page?

CHAPTER 6

Selling Accessibility

One of the hardest things about accessibility isn't necessarily implementing it; it's selling it. Why put all this effort into making your website accessible when it's such a small part of most sites' audience? Many website owners will be reluctant to delay a deployment or add more overhead to an existing project.

U.S. Government Requirement

If a company ever hopes to work on a contract for the U.S. government, it needs to be prepared to comply completely with 508 standards. The standards are required for nearly every web application (and desktop application) that is used in a government office. While this applies only to federal offices, state and local offices must also comply if they receive federal funds. Even if they don't, however, they still must comply with the Americans with Disabilities Act (ADA). Making a website accessible is rarely going to be considered an undue burden by official 508 testers, unless it is used by only one or two people.

Waivers, common years ago, are becoming more rare, and are now limited to applications that a disabled person would never use (for instance, a fighter jet), or the application is being built for a small audience that will never change (such as a selection committee for a one-time workshop). With reusability of applications being touted, the latter is becoming even more rare.

Non-U.S. Governments

What if a company doesn't do business with the U.S. government, but is considering the governments of other countries? Many foreign countries have used the 508 specifications as a template for their own rules of accessibility. Whatever country a disabled person is in, it doesn't change the fact that it can be difficult to use a computer if one is blind, has issues controlling a mouse, or can't hear the audio for a video.

Exclusion Can Hurt Your Business

Small business, such as family-owned restaurants or local shops, often don't consider how damaging not being compliant can be to their business. Let's say an owner of a pizza shop has a website for her shop, but has made a few accessibility mistakes.

First, she uses a Flash introduction (Figure 6-1). While this is annoying for most populations, this can be extremely detrimental to the blind, the physically impaired, or the cognitively impaired. Someone who is blind may not be able to load the Flash if his screen reader isn't set up for it. It might be overstimulating for someone with an information processing disorder. A physically disabled person may not be able to hit a Next button.

Figure 6-1. Flash Introduction

The menu, seen in Figure 6-2, is available only as a PDF, and this PDF is simply a scan of the printed menu. A blind user wouldn't be able to read it. A user with low vision might have trouble reading the scanned menu, since she can't make the text any larger or change the contrast. A user with dyslexia might have the same issues.

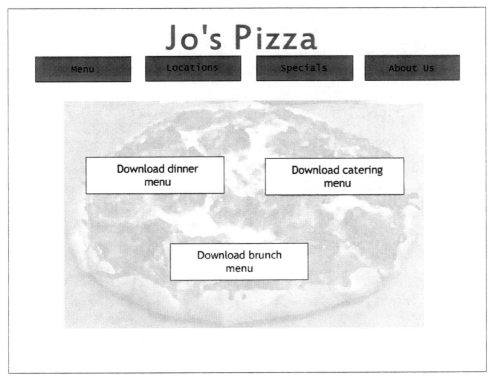

Figure 6-2. Inaccessible Menu

In Figure 6-3, the designer has chosen to display the addresses as images in order to more tightly control their styling. Without alt text, a blind user wouldn't be able to read the addresses. Once again, low vision and dyslexic users might be hurt by the inability to swap out colors or fonts, or grow the text.

- The front page has a Flash intro, at the end of which the user can click to enter the site. Unfortunately, there's no way to tab to this button.
- The front page also features the address of the shop, but this is included as a graphic that is missing alt text.
- The second page has a menu, but the menu is also a graphic.
- The business now offers online ordering, which is advertised through another graphic.

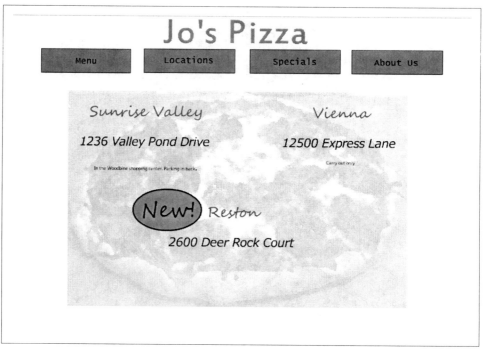

Figure 6-3. Graphics without alt text

Now, let's look at the people who can't interact with this website at all:

- People using their keyboard to navigate wouldn't be able to get past the front page.
- If the button is small, people with motion disorders might have trouble getting to the second page as well.
- People who are blind wouldn't be able to get the address of the shop, and depending on their screen reader, might not be able to make it to the second page.
- If a person who is blind makes it to the second page, they wouldn't know that they can order online and wouldn't be able to read the menu.

This is just a small list of fairly common errors, but this could exclude up to 10% of the potential traffic to the website.

An Accessible Site Is More Usable for Everyone

The effort to fix the pizza website would be minimal:

- Remove the Flash introduction page.
- Change the graphic of the address to text.
- Replace the graphical menu with a text menu.

- Add alt text to the online ordering graphic.

These changes make the site usable not only for the blind and motion-disabled, but for everyone.

Think of the example in Figure 6-2, and how our new website now appears to a typical user:

- The Flash intro is now gone, which was more than likely annoying to them.
- The address is now something they can copy-and-paste, which they might need to get directions to the shop's location.
- They no longer have to wait for a large graphic to load, which would be painful if they're trying to pull it up on a smart phone or on a slow connection.

The only change that didn't affect them directly was the online ordering graphic. A search engine, however, would have picked up the alt text and, if the alt text is being properly used, moved the site up in rankings. In the end, all of the changes end up helping the owner create a site that is less annoying to her customers and helped drive more customers to the website.

CHAPTER 7

Additional Resources

General Accessibility Resources

Table 7-1. 508 Resources

Site Name	URL	Description
Official U.S. Government website for 508 compliance	http://www.section508.gov/	Contains the official laws and policies around 508 compliance, as well as tools. Geared toward those creating websites for the U.S. government.
21st Century Communications and Accessibility Act	http://transition.fcc.gov/cgb/dro/cvaa .html/	A U.S. law building on section 508, focusing on new technologies. Expands beyond the Federal arena to consumer products.
WebAIM	http://webaim.org/	Articles, tools, and services for making accessible websites.
Penn State AccessAbility	http://accessibility.psu.edu/	Accessibility and usability at Penn State. Includes articles and practical examples for making accessible websites.
W3C's official page for accessibility	http://www.w3.org/standards/webde sign/accessibility/	Bullet points for why accessibility is important.
Paciello Group's blog	http://www.paciellogroup.com/blog/	Frequently updated blog on accessibility, tools, and standards.

Testing

Table 7-2. Browser tools

Tool	Browser	Description
Accessibility Developer Tools by Google	Chrome	Audits individual web pages for accessibility issues.

Tool	Browser	Description
N-WAX by mctenshi	Diagnoses basic usability issues on an individual webpage	
Chrome Shades by dmazzoni	Chrome	Tool built specifically for making sites more accessible for the blind. Pages are reformatted as text-only.
Chrome Daltonize	Chrome	Simulates common types of color blindness on websites.
Accessibility Evaluation Toolbar by Jon Gunderson	Firefox	Audits pages for accessibility issues.
Juicy Studio Accessibility Toolbar	Firefox	Evaluates WAI-ARIA areas in addition to other problem areas for accessibility.
WAVE Toolbar	Firefox	WebAIM's toolbar for diagnosing accessibility issues.
Fangs Screen Reader Emulator	Firefox	Displays the text that a screen reader would read to a user, as well as lists of headers and links.

Table 7-3. Websites

Site Name	URL	Description
W3C Validator	*http://validator.w3.org/*	Having proper mark up is vital for screen readers, so passing this validation is vital.
WAVE from WebAIM	*http://wave.webaim.org/*	Tests pages, uploaded files, and pasted HTML.
Cynthia Says	*http://www.cynthiasays.com/*	Checks individual pages. Can check against specific browsers.
EvalAccess	*http://sipt07.si.ehu.es/evalaccess2/index.html/*	Checks websites and individual pages.
Functional Accessibility Evaluator	*http://fae.cita.uiuc.edu/*	With registration, check entire websites.

Table 7-4. Applications

Site Name	URL	Description
Total Validator	*http://www.totalvalidator.com/*	Free desktop application for Linux, Windows, and Mac.
Accessibility features in Adobe Photoshop	*http://www.adobe.com/accessibility/products/photoshop/overview.html/*	How to use the accessibility features in CS6.
Creating accessible Flash features	*http://www.adobe.com/accessibility/products/flash/tutorial/*	Flash feature by Adobe, explaining Flash's accessibility features.

Design

Table 7-5. Design resources

Site Name	URL	Description
Color Scheme Designer	*http://colorschemedesigner.com/*	Allows user to see how a color scheme appears to those with various kinds of color blindness.
Daltonize	*http://www.vischeck.com/daltonize/runDaltonize.php/*	Make images more accessible to the color blind.
Vischeck	*http://www.vischeck.com/vischeck/vischeckURL.php/*	Show how images or a web page appear to various kinds of color blindness.
ColorBrewer	*http://colorbrewer2.org/*	Color blindness friendly color schemes for maps.
Google Web Fonts	*http://www.google.com/webfonts/*	Free, hosted web fonts.
Font Squirrel	*http://www.fontsquirrel.com/*	Free and commercial web fonts.
Font Spring	*http://www.fontspring.com/*	Pay-per-font, unlimited.
Typekit	*http://typekit.com/*	Subscription-based, limited page views.
Fonts.com	*http://www.fonts.com/web-fonts/*	Free, subscription- and fee-based, limited page views.

Screen Readers

Table 7-6. Available screen readers

Site Name	URL	Description
JAWS	*http://www.freedomscientific.com/products/fs/jaws-product-page.asp/*	Popular screen reader for Windows
NVDA	*http://www.nvda-project.org/*	Open source screen reader for Windows
Voice Over	*http://www.apple.com/accessibility/voiceover/*	Built-in screen reader for Mac
Orca	*https://live.gnome.org/Orca/*	Screen reader for Linux
ChromeVox	*https://chrome.google.com/webstore/detail/kgejglhpjiefppelpmljglcjbhoiplfn/*	Screen reader for Chrome

Hearing Disabled

Table 7-7. Resources for designing for hearing disabilities

Site Name	URL	Description
Adding captions to YouTube videos	*http://www.youtube.com/t/captions_about/*	Documentation on adding captions and notes to videos for the hearing impaired.
Universal Subtitles	*http://www.universalsubtitles.org/en/*	Tool for adding subtitles to any video (useful for services that don't support captioning).

Physically Disabled

Table 7-8. Tools overview

Site Name	URL	Description
Tools overview	*http://www.computerworld.com/s/article/9149058/14_tech_tools_that_enhance_computing_for_the_disabled/*	Overview of tools used by physically disabled to use computers.

Cognitively Disabled

Table 7-9. Tools for the cognitively disabled

Site Name	URL	Description
BrowseAloud	*http://www.browsealoud.com/*	Screen reader for those with dyslexia.
What dyslexics see	*http://uxmovement.com/content/6-surprising-bad-practices-that-hurt-dyslexic-users/*	Article on how certain design choices hurt those with dyslexia, with figures approximating what dyslexics might see.
Dyslexia Style Guide	*http://www.bdadyslexia.org.uk/about-dyslexia/further-information/dyslexia-style-guide.html/*	More information on designing for those with dyslexia.

About the Author

Katie Cunningham is a Python and Django developer for Cox Media Group. While she had always had an interest in programming, it didn't turn into a career until she started to work at NASA. There, she slowly transitioned from gathering requirements to developing full time, advocating the use of more open source in the government sector.

It was at NASA that she gained an interest in 508 compliance. At first, she was only interested in getting her applications through QA faster. Over time, however, she gained a passion for a web that was easy for everyone to use. Now in the private sector, she is championing compliance even for websites that don't require it by law.

Have it your way.

Get even more for your money.

Join the O'Reilly Community, and register the O'Reilly books you own. It's free, and you'll get:

- $4.99 ebook upgrade offer
- 40% upgrade offer on O'Reilly print books
- Membership discounts on books and events
- Free lifetime updates to ebooks and videos
- Multiple ebook formats, DRM FREE
- Participation in the O'Reilly community
- Newsletters
- Account management
- 100% Satisfaction Guarantee

Signing up is easy:

1. **Go to: oreilly.com/go/register**
2. **Create an O'Reilly login.**
3. **Provide your address.**
4. **Register your books.**

Note: English-language books only

To order books online:
oreilly.com/store

For questions about products or an order:
orders@oreilly.com

To sign up to get topic-specific email announcements and/or news about upcoming books, conferences, special offers, and new technologies:
elists@oreilly.com

For technical questions about book content:
booktech@oreilly.com

To submit new book proposals to our editors:
proposals@oreilly.com

O'Reilly books are available in multiple DRM-free ebook formats. For more information:
oreilly.com/ebooks

O'REILLY®

Spreading the knowledge of innovators   oreilly.com

CPSIA information can be obtained at www.ICGtesting.com
Printed in the USA
BVOW06s0056201213

339684BV00001B/2/P

9 781449 322854